*To my son, Sacha, for a brighter future:
Entrepreneurs forge tomorrow with today's innovations.
Through mindful AI application, we can steer a new
generation toward solving the pressing challenges
of our time, turning potential threats into opportunities
for progress.*

About the Author

From launching his first venture at 14 to pioneering AI-driven HR solutions, Paul Courtaud's journey embodies the essence of innovative entrepreneurship. His early start in the business world, with the creation of Fairlydeal, showcased his knack for blending commerce with social impact. This venture set the stage for a series of successful entrepreneurial pursuits, including co-founding Futurness at 16, a platform that redefined educational guidance.

Educated at prestigious institutions like HEC Lausanne, Sciences Po Paris, and later, Harvard University, Paul's academic path provided him a robust understanding of management, political science, and industrial organizational psychology. These experiences honed his insights into organizational dynamics and the importance of fostering environments that promote personal and professional growth.

At 22, Paul co-founded Neobrain, driven by a vision to navigate professional careers in a rapidly evolving job market. Under his leadership, Neobrain has flourished, gaining the trust of global giants like Safran, PwC, and LVMH. His role as co-president of Cercle Humania further amplifies his impact on human resources practices, sharing his deep knowledge and advocating for transformative HR strategies.

Paul's ventures into AI, from developing job market analytics at Futurness to pioneering skill-centered talent management at Neobrain, highlight his commitment to leveraging technology for progress. His optimistic outlook on AI's role in the future underscores a pressing need for adaptive learning and skill development to keep pace with market changes.

«Next-Gen AI Founders» is not just a reflection of Paul's journey but a manifesto for the future of entrepreneurship. Through this book, Paul shares a roadmap for harnessing AI to navigate the complexities of modern business, aiming to inspire a new generation of entrepreneurs to embrace innovation, continuous learning, and the transformative power of artificial intelligence.

Introduction

The dawn of AI-Enhanced Entrepreneurship

As I embark on the journey of writing «Next Gen AI Founders,» I'm acutely aware of the stark reality that entrepreneurship is akin to riding a relentless roller coaster. Even today, more than 70% of businesses falter within their first five years. The path of an entrepreneur is fraught with highs and lows, each turn bringing its own set of challenges and rewards. My intention with this book is to arm both budding and seasoned entrepreneurs with insights into how artificial intelligence (AI) is set to revolutionize the entrepreneurial landscape, offering not just a lifeline but a strategic advantage to reclaim their evenings and gain a broader perspective on their ventures.

This book comes to life in the months leading up to the arrival of my first child, a time that has inspired me to harness my creativity and lean on AI to save time and gain insights. It's these discoveries, born from necessity and innovation, that I'm eager to share with you. Beyond personal productivity, I'm convinced that the next five years will see a dramatic reshuffling of the business deck. AI is lowering barriers to entry and threatening to sweep away the less resilient businesses, including some of the largest incumbents. This shift presents a golden opportunity for entrepreneurs eyeing the AI market, projected to be worth no less than $300 billion by 2024, with an average growth rate of 15.83% from 2024 to 2030.

In writing this book, I bring not just the lessons learned from my own ventures, from Fairlydeal to Neobrain, but also a humble perspective. Success in entrepreneurship, as in life, is never guaranteed, and the journey is often more about resilience and learning from failures than about celebrating victories. My academic and professional experiences, from HEC Lausanne to Sciences Po Paris, and finally, Harvard University, have taught me the importance of humility in the face of success and the value of perseverance through challenges.

The first part of our journey, «AI Capabilities Unleashed,» will demystify AI for you, breaking down the myths and revealing the realities. We'll explore the inner workings of AI, the milestones that marked 2023 as a tipping point, and the ethical considerations that must guide our innovations. This foundational knowledge is crucial not just for understanding AI but for envisioning its potential to transform our world.

As we move to «AI to Augment Yourself and Your Business,» I aim to translate the theoretical into the practical. This section is about tangible applications of AI that can transform the way you work, innovate, and grow your business. From optimizing your time to redefining product development and customer experiences, AI can be your most valuable ally in the entrepreneurial journey.

Finally, «Build Your Business in the AI Arena» is a call to action. It's about recognizing the immense opportunities within the AI market and understanding how to navigate, innovate, and thrive within it. This part of the book is designed to guide you through launching and scaling an AI venture, drawing on the lessons from my own experiences and the projected growth of the AI industry.

«Next Gen AI Founders» is more than just a guide; it's a reflection on the transformative power of AI in entrepreneurship and a personal narrative of innovation and adaptation. Welcome to the dawn of AI-enhanced entrepreneurship, where the future is not just written but engineered.

Let's begin.

1

AI capabilities unleashed

Chapter 1

Introduction to the Next Gen AI Founders Mastery Scale

Throughout this book, we will frequently reference a scale designed to help you self-assess your mastery of AI. This scale isn't just a measure of knowledge, but a reflection of your capacity to leverage AI within a business context. As a startup founder, it's not necessary to become a technical expert in AI, but understanding its capabilities, limitations, and applications can significantly empower your decision-making and strategic planning.

To remain competitive and innovative in today's market, a founder should aim to reach at least level 7 on this scale. This level represents a robust understanding of AI's potential and practical implications, allowing for strategic integration of AI technologies within their business models. Keep in mind that this scale is a tool for self-evaluation, designed to help you identify where you stand and what areas to focus on for improvement.

The AI Mastery Scale

1. **AI Novice:** You're aware of AI and its buzz in the market but have no understanding of how it works or its applications.

2. **AI Observer:** You recognize AI's impact in various sectors and have a general sense of its potential, though you haven't engaged with it directly.

3. **AI Enthusiast:** You actively follow AI trends and have a basic understanding of AI concepts like machine learning and data analytics.

4. **AI Apprentice:** You've experimented with AI tools or taken introductory courses, grasping foundational concepts and their practical uses.

5. **AI Implementer:** You can apply AI solutions for business problems and have a grasp of different AI technologies and their potential ROI.

6. **AI Strategist:** You can develop strategies that incorporate AI, understanding its broader business implications and ethical considerations.

7. **AI Integrator:** You're proficient in aligning AI capabilities with business goals, effectively integrating AI solutions into operations and processes.

8. **AI Innovator:** You understand advanced AI concepts and can drive innovation, oversee AI projects, and comprehend the nuances of AI integration.

9. **AI Thought Leader:** You contribute to AI discussions, predict trends, and influence the direction of AI in your industry.

10. **AI Visionary:** You possess a deep understanding of AI's frontier technologies and can shape future AI advancements in the global market.

Remember, the goal isn't to become an AI technician, but rather to understand AI well enough to make informed decisions and keep pace with the rapid advancements in the field. As we delve into AI myths and realities, consider where you currently land on this scale and where you aim to be by the end of this book.

AI Myths vs. Reality

To start with, the first requirement for Next-Gen AI founders... is AI. You need to avoid the most common myths and be able to explain and debate AI. With these six myths versus reality, you'll be armed to shine in society.

Myth #1 AI's Agency

The concept of AI having agency is a common misconception and is often perpetuated by sensationalist headlines in the media. The notion that AI can act independently, have desires, or make autonomous decisions is incorrect. Instead, AI systems are tools created and utilized by humans to perform specific tasks based on pre-programmed algorithms and data provided by humans.

A critical look at the way AI is presented in headlines reveals that it's not the AI itself designing cities or developing drugs but rather teams of researchers and engineers using AI tools to analyze data and generate results. This distinction is crucial because it demystifies the technology and grounds it in reality, highlighting the human agency behind AI systems.

Anthropomorphizing AI can be misleading, making it seem as if the technology operates without human intervention, which can obscure the important ethical and practical considerations involved in its development and deployment. For instance, if an AI system is used for urban planning, it is essential to ask whether the dataset it was trained on is representative of the population's diversity. Failure to address this can lead to biased outcomes, such as the perpetuation of gentrification.

Moreover, referring to AI as if it has agency can hide the human labor that goes into its operation, a phenomenon sometimes referred to as «fauxtomation.» This term describes situations where the manual and often underpaid work that supports AI, such as data labeling or moderating content, is overlooked. By recognizing that these systems are part of «sociotechnical ensembles,» we can better understand and address the myriad of human decisions that shape AI technologies.

In more concerning cases, the supposed autonomy of AI can mask serious issues, such as the human review of recordings from voice assistants like Siri or Alexa. Users might not be aware that their interactions with these devices are sometimes reviewed by humans to improve the system, which raises privacy concerns.

The anthropomorphization and gendering of AI assistants can also create problematic perceptions, making users feel like they are interacting with an intelligent being rather than a programmed system supported by extensive human labor.

HEADLINE #3	REPHRASING #3
Artificial intelligence news: Brain-based AI discovers "remarkable" antibiotic Source: aimyths.org	Pharmaceutical news: scientists make use of machine learning system to help in dicovering a new antibiotic

<table>
<tr>
<td>

HEADLINE #5

People are using artificial intelligence to help sort out their divorce. Would you?

Source: aimyths.org

</td>
<td>

REPHRASING #5

Because the Australian legal system is overburdened ans legal costs are so high, people are being urged to use a cheap-fix, simplistic chatbot solution to provide legal advice in the complex situation of divorce. Would you?

</td>
</tr>
<tr>
<td>

HEADLINE #4

Artificial intelligence Can Now Write Amazing Content – What Does That Mean For Humans?

Source: aimyths.org

</td>
<td>

REPHRASING #4

People can use computer programs to make barely passable imitations of generic written content provided they have enormous numbers of examples, but they are liable to say horrible racist and sexist things - what does that mean for humans?

</td>
</tr>
</table>

These examples illustrate the crucial role of human agency in AI systems' functioning and decision-making processes. They show that, contrary to some narratives, AI does not operate with autonomy or intentionality but as a tool under human direction.

In summary, AI does not have agency. It is a human-created and human-directed technology that relies on human input and operates. within the scope of its programming and the data it has been fed. It's important to communicate about AI in a way that reflects its true nature and the human labor behind it, avoiding misconceptions that can lead to ethical oversights and the underappreciation of the human work that makes AI possible.

Myth #2   AI Can Surpass Human Intelligence Imminently

The narrative that artificial intelligence (AI) is on the brink of surpassing human intelligence is widespread, stirring both fascination and fear. This myth, often referred to as the advent of «superintelligence,» suggests that machines will soon develop cognitive abilities that outstrip our own, potentially leading to scenarios where humans are no longer in control.

At its core, this myth misconstrues the nature and current capabilities of AI. Today's AI systems excel at specific, narrow tasks, such as image recognition, playing strategic games, or analyzing large datasets to identify patterns. These systems operate under a framework defined by human programmers, relying on vast amounts of data to «learn» and make decisions within their specified domain.

The distinction between narrow AI (or weak AI) and general AI (or strong AI) is crucial here. All existing AI systems are narrow AI, optimized for specific tasks without the consciousness, understanding, or versatility of human intelligence. General AI, a theoretical concept, would possess the ability to understand, learn, and apply knowledge across a wide range of tasks, mimicking human cognitive abilities. Despite progress in AI research, the creation of general AI remains a speculative and distant goal.

AI's current success stories often overshadow the indispensable role of human oversight and decision-making. For instance, medical diagnosis AI can sift through thousands of images to spot diseases with remarkable accuracy. However, the final judgment and treatment plan rest with medical professionals, who consider the AI's analysis alongside a patient's broader medical history and personal circumstances.

Ray Kurzweil's prediction that AI will achieve human-level intelligence by 2029, measured by passing the Turing Test, is a provocative statement that sparks much debate. The Turing Test, devised by Alan Turing in 1950, assesses a machine's intelligence based on its ability to imitate human behavior indistinguishably. However, this benchmark is seen by many, including machine learning researcher François Chollet, as inadequate for truly gauging 'human-level intelligence.' Chollet argues that intelligence is inherently task-specific and context-dependent, emphasizing that current AI excels only in narrowly defined tasks. This viewpoint challenges the notion that simply enhancing computational power will lead to a general, human-like intelligence, suggesting instead that intelligence must be understood within the specific problems it aims to solve and its cultural and environmental context.

Predictions about AI surpassing human intelligence any time soon are speculative at best. The AI field faces numerous challenges, including ethical considerations, data bias, and the limitations of current technology, which must be addressed to advance safely and responsibly.

The myth of imminent superintelligence overlooks the nuanced reality of AI development. While AI's capabilities are impressive and growing, they remain tools—albeit sophisticated ones—that amplify human effort. The journey toward general AI, if it ever occurs, is much longer and complex than sensational headlines suggest. For entrepreneurs, this underscores the importance of leveraging AI as a partner to human ingenuity, not a replacement.

Myth #3 **AI, Machine Learning, Deep Learning and GenAI are all the same thing**

These concepts can be explained in 1,000 more or less technical ways. I'm going to use a garden metaphor to help you better understand the interweaving of these different concepts. With this first level of mastery, you'll be able to better grasp the dynamics of the AI market, its bottlenecks and its potential.

Imagine stepping into a vast, lush garden—this is the world of Artificial Intelligence (AI). Within this garden, there are various paths you can follow, each leading to different realms of understanding and capability. This garden is designed to mimic the complexity and adaptability of human intelligence, but each path represents a different approach to achieving this goal.

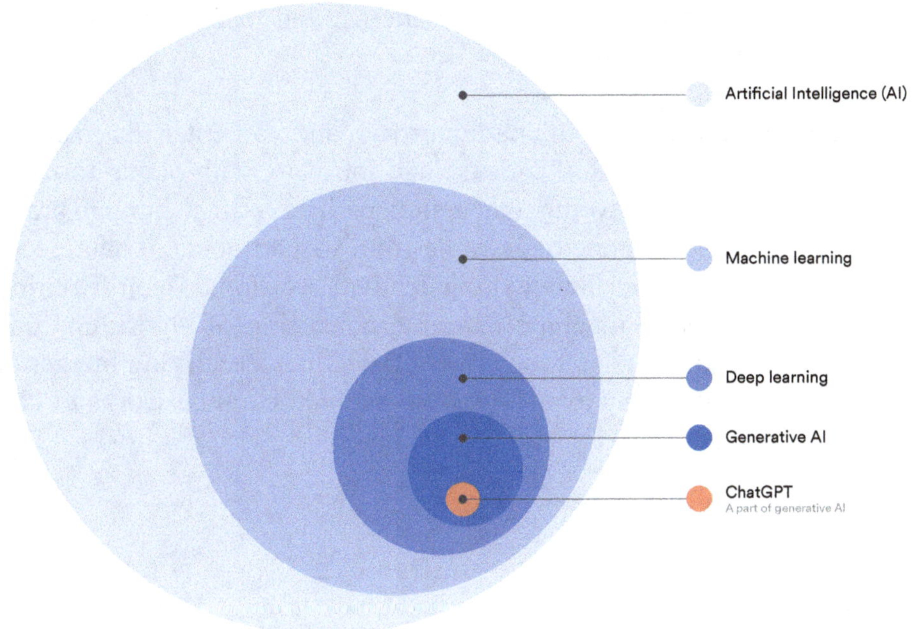

The AI Spectrum: Unveiling Layers of Intelligent Systems

① The Garden's Main Paths: AI, ML, and Deep Learning

Artificial Intelligence is the entire garden itself, a sprawling expanse of possibilities where technology is cultivated to think, learn, and act in a way that mimics human intelligence. It's the overarching concept that covers all efforts to create machines capable of interpreting data, making decisions, and performing tasks that would typically require human intellect.

As you walk further, you come across a more defined path, Machine Learning. This path is where the garden's plants learn to grow and adapt by themselves, without a gardener's constant supervision. Here, the plants are given examples of how to flourish, and over time, they learn from these examples, figuring out the best way to thrive in various conditions on their own. **Machine learning** is the process of teaching computers to learn from data, recognize patterns, and make decisions with minimal human intervention.

Deeper into the garden, the path narrows, and you enter the realm of Deep Learning. This section is dense and intricate, with plants forming complex networks, mirroring the neural pathways in a human brain. These networks are capable of learning from vast amounts of data, recognizing intricate patterns, and making detailed decisions. **Deep learning** represents a subset of machine learning, consisting of algorithms that enable software to train itself to perform tasks, like identifying images or understanding speech, by exposing multilayered neural networks to vast amounts of data.

The Newest Addition: Generative AI

Beyond the dense foliage of deep learning, you discover a new, vibrant area of the garden: Generative AI. This part of the garden is magical; not only do the plants grow and adapt, but they also start creating new plants on their own. Generative AI is akin to giving the garden the power to dream up and cultivate entirely new species of plants that never existed before, using the genetic makeup of existing plants as a blueprint. This technology can generate new content, ideas, or data that mimic original examples, producing everything from new images, texts, and music that feel remarkably human-made.

In this garden, AI represents the fertile ground of possibility; machine learning is the process by which the garden learns to tend to itself; deep learning is the dense, interconnected network of roots and branches that empower the garden with deep knowledge; and Generative AI is the magical capability of the garden to create new life forms on its own. Each concept builds upon the last, illustrating the layered and evolving nature of artificial intelligence. Through this metaphor, we can appreciate the complexity and beauty of AI and its potential to transform our world.

Myth #4　AI as the Inscrutable "Black Box"

The «black box» myth perpetuates the idea that all artificial intelligence (AI) systems are inherently opaque, their inner workings shrouded in mystery beyond human comprehension. This myth suggests that AI's decision-making process is far less explainable than that of non-AI systems or even human reasoning. However, this isn't an accurate reflection of the AI landscape.

1　AI Spectrum of Transparency

AI's explainability spans a broad spectrum. On one end, we have simple AI systems whose logic can be as transparent as a glass pane. For example, a basic decision tree algorithm used for sorting emails into categories is easy to follow: if an email contains certain keywords, it goes to the «Promotions» folder; otherwise, it lands in «Primary.» Here, the «why» behind the AI's decision is clear and traceable.

On the other end, complex deep learning networks with millions of parameters are harder to interpret. These systems, often criticized as «black boxes,» process information in ways that are not immediately clear to even their creators. Yet, the field of explainable AI (XAI) is making strides in developing methods and tools to shed light on these opaque processes.

② Concrete Examples of Non-«Black Box» AI

Medical Imaging Analysis:

A convolutional neural network (CNN) can identify diseases from medical images, such as X-rays. Tools from XAI can create heat maps that highlight areas of the image most influential in the CNN's decision. This helps medical professionals understand why the AI flagged a particular scan as abnormal, ensuring the AI's recommendations are reliable and actionable.

Credit Scoring Models:

Some AI models used by financial institutions for credit scoring are designed for high interpretability. They provide scores based on a clear set of criteria—such as payment history, credit utilization, and length of credit history. These models can also offer explanations for a credit score, such as «Your score is lower because of your high credit card balances.»

③ The Advantages of AI in Decision Transparency

Interestingly, AI can sometimes offer greater transparency in decision-making than humans. Human decisions are often influenced by unconscious biases and emotional states that are difficult to articulate or even recognize. In contrast, an AI system's decision-making process can be recorded and analyzed. With the right tools, we can review the specific data points and model characteristics that led to a given AI decision. This level of scrutiny is rarely possible with human decision-makers.

Dismissing all AI as «black boxes» ignores the diversity of AI systems and the progress being made in XAI. By understanding and improving the explainability of AI, we can harness its potential to enhance decision-making transparency in critical areas such as healthcare, finance, and beyond. As AI continues to evolve, so too does our ability to peer into the «black box,» ensuring AI remains a tool that can be trusted and understood.

Myth #5 **AI is only as good as the data on which it has been trained**

The common belief that an AI system is only as good as the data it's trained on oversimplifies the intricate tapestry of artificial intelligence. Indeed, data is a critical component, but it's not the sole ingredient that determines the quality of an AI system. There's a quartet of elements essential for AI innovation: data, algorithms, computing hardware, and human expertise. Let's unpack this myth and explore how AI isn't held captive by its training data.

The Four Pillars of AI Innovation

1. **Data:** It's the raw material, the fuel for the AI engine. However, perfection is unattainable in real-world datasets — they're often incomplete, unbalanced, or noisy.

2. **Algorithms:** These are the engines of AI, becoming increasingly sophisticated to make the most out of available data, whether it's plenty or sparse.

3. **Hardware:** The muscle behind the mind, hardware accelerates computation, allowing for more complex models and quicker iteration.

4. **Human Talent:** The maestros conducting the AI symphony, human experts craft, tune, and innovate, turning data and algorithms into solutions.

Addressing Imperfect Data

AI doesn't throw in the towel when faced with imperfect data. Here are some concrete examples of how AI systems can rise above data limitations:

1. **Targeted Sampling:** Suppose we're dealing with a medical diagnosis AI that's trained on a dataset with an overrepresentation of one demographic. By employing targeted sampling, we ensure a more diverse dataset, improving the model's accuracy and fairness across different patient groups.

2. **Synthetic Data:** In autonomous vehicle development, encountering every possible driving scenario is impractical. By generating synthetic data—virtual simulations of rare or dangerous driving conditions—developers can train AI systems to handle these scenarios without putting anyone at risk.

3. **Building Constraints into Models:** When training an AI for financial fraud detection, the data might be overwhelmingly 'normal' transactions. By building constraints into the model, it can focus on learning the subtle patterns indicative of fraud, despite their rarity in the dataset.

Let's simplify, imagine an orchestra. The data is the sheet music, algorithms are the instruments, hardware is the concert hall's acoustics, and human talent is the conductor. If the sheet music has a few missing notes (imperfect data), a skilled conductor (AI expert) can still lead the orchestra (AI system) to a stellar performance, improvising and adapting as needed.

To say an AI's prowess is bound solely by its training data is to ignore the symphony of elements at play in AI innovation. Through the ingenious blend of algorithms, computing power, and human ingenuity, AI can transcend the limitations of its training data, continually reshaping the boundaries of what's possible.

Myth #6 ## AI can solve any problem

While AI and machine learning (ML) have made significant strides in addressing complex issues, it's a myth that AI can solve any problem. There are clear limits to what machine learning can achieve, and understanding these is crucial to setting realistic expectations for the technology.

We're going to focus here on the three limits you need to be aware of in order to better understand which problems are addressable and which are not.

① **Perception Problems:** ML has shown progress in areas where there is a clear ground truth to measure against, such as speech-to-text transcription and facial verification. With enough data, computing power, and meticulous algorithmic design, AI can learn to distinguish between different inputs to a high degree of accuracy. Yet, this doesn't mean that AI can solve any perception problem. There are still challenges related to data quality, ethical considerations, and the complexities of the real world that can hinder AI's effectiveness.

② **Automating Judgment:** When it comes to automating judgment, like in spam detection or hate speech identification, the success of AI varies greatly. In scenarios where there is a general consensus on what constitutes a specific category, like spam, AI can achieve high accuracy. However, in more subjective areas, such as determining what is considered hate speech, definitions are contentious and nuanced, making it difficult for AI to make accurate judgments.

③ **Predicting Social Outcomes:** The most challenging area for AI is predicting social outcomes, such as criminal recidivism or job performance. These problems combine contentious criteria with the uncertainty of predicting future events. For instance, the Fragile Families & Child Wellbeing Study, which aimed to predict life outcomes based on extensive data, showed that ML algorithms did not perform significantly better than much simpler models. This underscores the fact that complex social phenomena cannot be accurately predicted using historical data alone, and attempting to do so can lead to harmful outcomes due to oversimplification and bias.

Additionally, relying on AI to predict social outcomes introduces risks such as the invasion of privacy, transferring power to tech companies without accountability, and the illusion of objectivity, which can distract from more effective social interventions.

Concrete examples of AI's limitations include the COMPAS recidivism prediction system, which was shown to be no more accurate than predictions made by people with minimal criminal justice expertise. Moreover, the use of AI in trying to predict 'criminality' from facial images has been widely condemned as pseudoscientific and biased.

In conclusion, while AI is a powerful tool, it is not a panacea for all problems. Certain tasks may be well-suited to AI solutions, but many complex, subjective, and socially significant issues require human judgment, ethical considerations, and a broader approach than what AI can currently offer.

What does Machine Learning excel at?

Machine learning excels in various areas that can significantly enhance our daily lives. It proves especially effective in tasks that are challenging for humans, such as meticulously analyzing vast quantities of text or video data to detect specific words or items. Equally, machine learning is adept at handling activities that, despite human proficiency, might not be desirable for us to perform due to their monotonous or distressing nature.

Consider the task of language translation. While human experts excel in this field, and most people have the potential to learn another language, automated tools like Google Translate offer instant translations that are sufficiently accurate for everyday needs. While these translations won't rival the nuanced work of skilled literary translators, they efficiently handle everyday translations, such as understanding a foreign menu while traveling.

Furthermore, machine learning can be employed for tasks that are deemed objectionable or particularly distasteful. For example, a machine learning system developed by Stanford researchers was trained to identify individuals by their unique 'analprint' for health monitoring purposes. The concept of manually learning and verifying someone's identity by such intimate means is understandably uncomfortable for most. However, it's a relief to note that there are far less intrusive identity verification methods available, like fingerprint recognition, which highlight the importance of considering ethical and privacy concerns when designing such systems.

Chapter 3
The Mechanics of Large Language Models: How Does It Work?

Despite their complexity, large language models operate on relatively simple principles. They are rooted in statistics and use probabilities to predict the next sequence of text. For instance, if you were to train a large language model on all the plays written by Shakespeare (Mira Murati - OpenAI CTO example), it would analyze the sequence of letters in those plays to predict what comes next based on a table of probabilities.

After: S

Table of probabilities

Source: Code. org

Initially, this approach may produce gibberish. The key to achieving coherence lies in training the model to consider a sequence of letters or even sentences, providing it a richer context. This is where neural networks come into play.

The Role of Neural Networks

A neural network is a computational model inspired by the human brain's neural structure. Instead of a simple table of probabilities, it utilizes a more complex system that can learn from its training data. In the context of large language models, these neural networks consider a broad sequence to predict the next best letter or token, improving the model's capability to produce meaningful text.

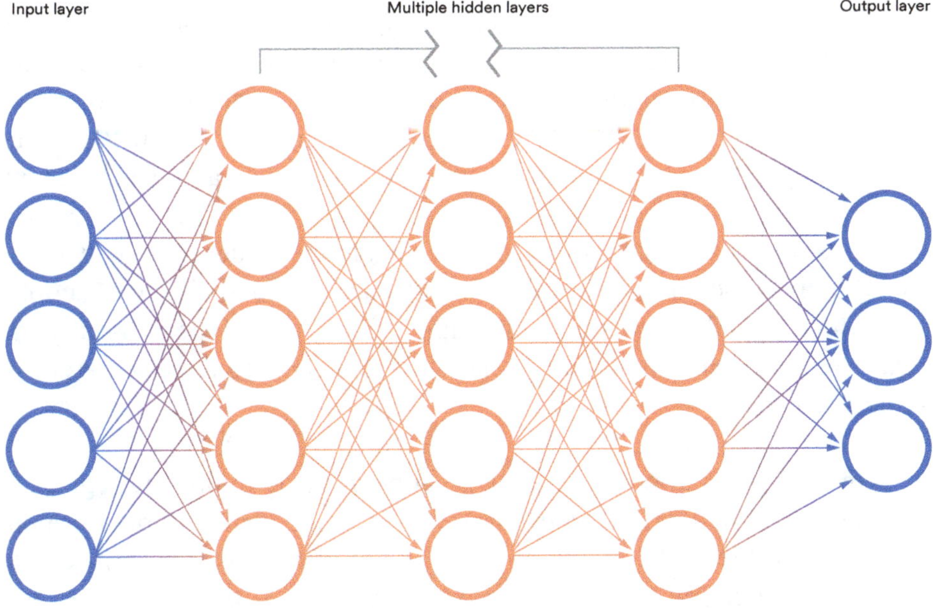

Deep neutral network
Source: IBM

What Sets ChatGPT Apart according to Mira?

ChatGPT is unique in three significant ways:

1 It is trained on a massive dataset that includes virtually all the information available on the Internet.

2 Instead of focusing on just the 26 alphabets, it predicts tokens, which can be full words, parts of words, or even code.

3 It undergoes extensive human tuning to produce reasonable and safe content while mitigating the risk of generating biased or dangerous information.

Tokens: The Building Blocks of Intelligent Text Generation

Think of tokens in generative AI like the building blocks of a Lego castle. In the same way you'd piece together different Lego blocks to create structures, a generative AI uses tokens to construct sentences or paragraphs. A token can be as small as a single letter or as long as an entire word. Just like each Lego block has a specific shape and function, each token has specific linguistic properties that help the AI understand and generate text.

For example, let's say you want to generate the sentence «ChatGPT is cool.» In this case, the tokens might be [«ChatGPT», « «, «is», « «, «cool», «.»]. The AI would use its understanding of how these tokens usually appear in relation to one another to generate this specific sentence or to create similar sentences.

Why are tokens important? Well, imagine trying to build that Lego castle without having the right types of blocks. It would be incredibly difficult, if not impossible. Tokens give the AI the 'building materials' it needs to construct meaningful and accurate text. They allow it to break down complex tasks into manageable pieces, analyze those pieces, and then put them back together in a coherent way.

So, just like you can't build a Lego castle without individual blocks, a generative AI can't generate text without tokens. They're the essential building blocks that make the whole process work.

Shortcomings and Ethical Considerations

Despite the advanced capabilities, it's crucial to remember that large language models can and do get things wrong. They are not genuinely «intelligent» in the way humans are; they are probability machines that can produce amazing yet imperfect results.

They'll say it better than I can...

- "It's important to note that this system is still just using random probabilities to choose words." - Mira Murati, CTO at OpenAI.

- "A large language model can produce unbelievable results that seem like magic, but because it's not actually magic, it can often get things wrong." - Cristóbal Valenzuela, CEO of Runway.

The Future of AI

As both Mira and Cristóbal pointed out, the advancements in AI have far-reaching implications. From creating applications to discovering new drugs, the applications are endless. While debates continue on whether these models exhibit real intelligence, there is no denying their transformative power.

My Humble Opinion: The Evolving Landscape of Generative AI

Democratising AI through Chatbots

Generative AI, and particularly OpenAI's ChatGPT interface, has played a pivotal role in democratizing access to artificial intelligence. Whether you're brainstorming gift ideas or cooking up new recipes, ChatGPT makes it easier for everyone to understand the possible applications of AI. It's bringing the power of machine learning into everyday conversations, breaking down barriers and inspiring innovative uses.

The Future Lies in a Symphony of Narrow AIs

In my opinion, the next two years will be crucial for AI development, and success will come from combining various Narrow AIs, each tailored for specific tasks. The amalgamation of automated or AI-augmented tasks will open up new applications that we're just beginning to explore. For example, with tools like Zapier, ChatGPT, and Midjourney, one can automate the creation of an e-commerce site, manage SEO, grow an Instagram community, and automate sales and support. In the HR realm, a matching model can be combined with generative AI to offer transparent explanations, thus integrating two AIs with complementary skills.

Proceed with Caution

While I'm generally optimistic about the prospects of AI and the conveniences it will bring, I believe that a lack of understanding of its limitations can lead to disastrous outcomes. The phenomenon of AI 'hallucination' is one such limitation that I'll delve into in a future article. I've observed many software vendors in the HR industry indiscriminately applying generative AI to cash in on the hype. Instead, we should be using AI cautiously and for specific use-cases where it genuinely adds value.

The Ethical and Societal Implications of AI

In this chapter, we delve deeper into the ethical and societal implications of artificial intelligence (AI), focusing on its progressive impact on education, sociology, and employment, alongside the crucial aspect of regulation. AI's influence extends far beyond the realms of technology and business, shaping the very fabric of society, our educational paradigms, and the global job market. Understanding these impacts is essential for navigating the ethical considerations and societal shifts AI brings.

Transparency and Accountability

Transparency and accountability in AI are paramount, especially as AI systems begin to play a more significant role in critical decision-making processes. The ethical imperative to ensure AI decisions are understandable and accountable is highlighted by the challenges posed by «black box» algorithms, particularly in sectors like criminal justice and healthcare, where lives and livelihoods can hang in the balance.

Bias and Fairness

The issue of bias in AI underscores the importance of ethically sourced, unbiased training data. Bias in AI not only perpetuates existing societal inequalities but can also amplify them, affecting everything from facial recognition technology to job screening processes. Initiatives like IBM's toolkit for detecting and mitigating bias in AI models represent steps toward addressing these challenges, yet the journey toward truly unbiased AI is ongoing and complex.

Transforming Education

Drawing upon insights from a comprehensive McKinsey study on the evolving dynamics of teachers' roles in education, it's clear that Artificial Intelligence (AI) and automation are set to revolutionize the educational landscape. As educators grapple with the dual pressures of administrative duties and the need for direct student engagement, AI emerges as a pivotal tool in reshaping priorities and practices within the classroom. The study, which surveyed over 2,000 teachers across Canada, Singapore, the United Kingdom, and the United States, underscores a crucial trend: teachers are currently bogged down by preparation, evaluation, and administrative tasks, significantly curtailing the time available for direct interaction with students.

Teachers work about 50 hours a week, spending less than half of the time in direct interaction with students.

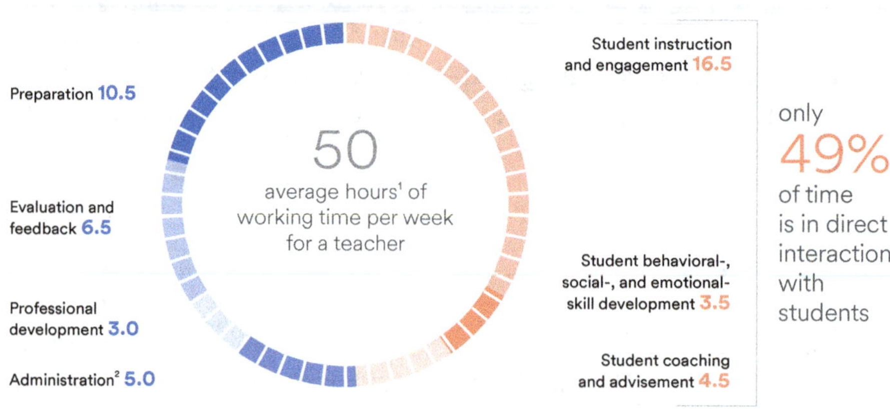

Activity composition of teacher working hours, number of hours

Source: McKinsey Global Teacher and Student Survey
1 Average for respondents in Canada, Singapore, United Kingdom, and United States. 2 Includes a small «other» category.

However, AI and technology offer a beacon of hope. By automating the more mundane and time-consuming tasks, such as lesson preparation, grading, and administrative paperwork, AI is poised to free up a substantial portion of teachers' time. Specifically, the study estimates that effective use of technology could reduce the time spent on preparation activities alone from an average of 11 hours a week to just six. This newfound time can be redirected towards activities that have a direct impact on student learning and personal development, including personalized instruction, mentoring, and coaching.

The positive implications of this shift are manifold. First, it enables teachers to devote more energy to facilitating a learning environment that caters to the individual needs of each student, thus enhancing the quality of education. Personalized learning, supported by AI-driven insights, allows educators to tailor their teaching strategies to the unique learning styles and requirements of their students, fostering a more inclusive and effective educational experience.

Technology can help teachers reallocate 20 to 30 percent of their timetoward activities that support student learning.

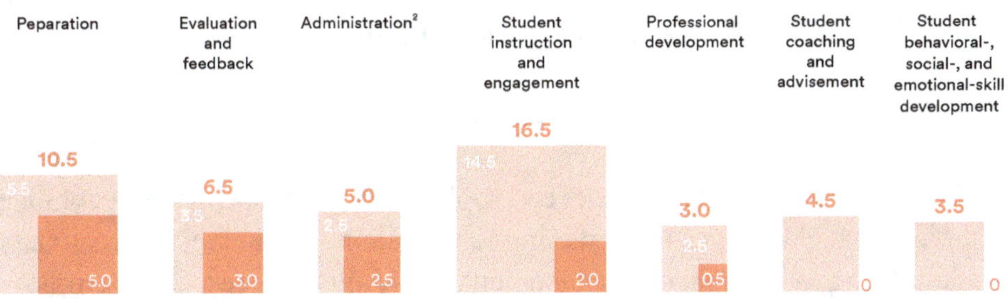

Potential for time reallocation, number of hours per week1

Source: McKinsey Global Teacher and Student Survey
1 Figures may not sum, because of rounding. Average for respondents in canada, Singapore, United Kingdom, and United States.2 Includes a small «other» category.

Moreover, by transitioning from the traditional role of content deliverer to that of a facilitator and coach, teachers can cultivate a more interactive and engaging classroom environment. This approach not only bolsters student learning outcomes but also elevates the role of teachers, emphasizing their critical importance in guiding and mentoring students. The McKinsey study further suggests that the time saved through automation could be invested in more personalized learning approaches, which have been identified by teachers themselves as a key area for improvement.

In summary, AI's impact on education extends beyond mere efficiency gains. It heralds a significant shift in the role of teachers, enabling them to focus on what truly matters: fostering deep, meaningful connections with their students, and preparing them for a future where adaptability, critical thinking, and personal growth are paramount. This transition, facilitated by AI, not only enhances the quality of education but also elevates the teaching profession, making it more rewarding and impactful.

Shifting Sociological Dynamics

AI is reshaping societal structures, influencing everything from social interactions to cultural norms. The proliferation of AI in daily life alters how individuals connect, communicate, and perceive the world around them. Sociological research points to both the potential for increased global connectivity and the risk of deepening social divides. As AI becomes more embedded in social systems, it is vital to consider its implications on human behavior, community, and societal norms.

The Evolution of Employment

When considering AI's impact on employment, it is essential to recognize our historical challenges in predicting job creation. While we've been adept at identifying jobs at risk of displacement, our ability to foresee new employment opportunities has been less accurate. According to a recent Goldman Sachs study, 60% of current occupations did not exist 80 years ago, highlighting how technology and new business models have historically created more opportunities than they've displaced. However, the concern remains that the jobs created may not be geographically aligned with those that are lost, as illustrated by the potential for AI technologies like voice-operated systems to automate call centers in regions such as Madagascar.

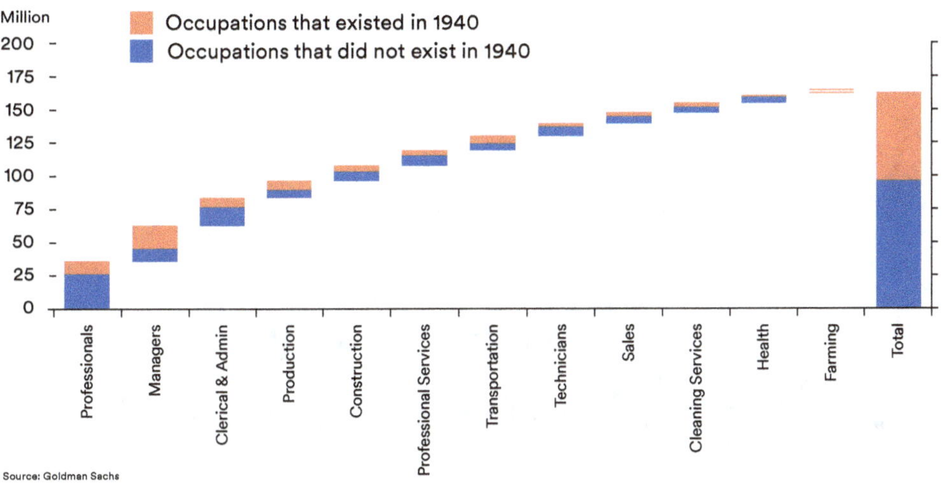

Source: Goldman Sachs

Global Regulation and Local Challenges

While the EU AI Act represents a significant step towards regulating AI's ethical use, the challenge of AI regulation is inherently global. The local or regional approach to AI governance may not suffice in addressing the global nature of employment challenges and technological impacts. The need for a coordinated, international framework for AI regulation is becoming increasingly apparent, as the effects of AI transcend borders, raising questions about global equity, access, and standards.

The ethical and societal implications of AI demand a nuanced, informed approach. As AI continues to shape education, alter sociological structures, and transform the employment landscape, the need for ethical guidelines, equitable access, and global regulatory frameworks has never been more critical. By addressing these challenges head-on, we can harness AI's potential to benefit society while mitigating its risks, ensuring a future where technology serves humanity, enhancing our collective capabilities and fostering a more inclusive world.

Chapter 5
Quizz - What do you understand about AI?

As we wrap up Part I - «AI Capabilities Unleashed», let's put your newfound knowledge to the test. This 20-question quiz is designed to gauge your understanding of AI concepts and their applications. Your responses will help you self-assess and identify where you might fall on the Next Gen AI Founders Mastery Scale we discussed earlier. It's not just about getting the right answers—it's about reflecting on how AI can be integrated into your entrepreneurial journey.

As you take this quiz, write down the letters of your answers and find the correction at the end of the book with the interpretation, including your positioning on the «Next-Gen AI Founder» scale.

Ready to see how well you know AI? Let's begin.

What does AI stand for?

A • Artificial Intelligence
B • Artificial Invention
C • Automated Intellect

Name one key difference between AI and machine learning

A • AI is a broader concept that includes ML
B • ML can function without AI
C • There is no difference

Can AI operate without data? Yes/No—Explain why

A • No, data is essential for AI to learn and make predictions
B • Yes, AI can make decisions based on pre-programmed rules
C • Yes, AI can operate on intuition

What is deep learning's main architectural inspiration?

A • The structure of the human brain
B • The behavior of ants
C • The growth patterns of plants

Identify one task that machine learning performs better than traditional programming

A • Predictive analysis
B • Creating simple arithmetic calculations
C • Writing novels

True or False: AI can make decisions based on emotions like humans

A • True
B • False

What does 'training' an AI model involve?

A • Giving it a strict set of instructions to follow
B • Exposing it to large datasets to learn from patterns
C • Regular maintenance checks like a machine

Give an example of a task that AI can automate in a business setting

A • Scheduling appointments
B • Negotiating business deals
C • Making coffee

Name one limitation of AI in its current state

A • It can't experience human emotions
B • It is always 100% accurate
C • It has replaced all human jobs

What is the Turing Test designed to evaluate?

A • The strength of a computer's hardware
B • T-An AI's ability to exhibit intelligent behavior equivalent
   to a human
C • The speed of a computer's processor

Describe one ethical consideration when implementing AI

A • Ensuring it has a sleek design
B • Making it affordable for consumers
C • Preventing bias in AI algorithms

Can AI create new content on its own? How?

A • No, it can only use existing content
B • Yes, by learning from data and generating patterns
C • Yes, by dreaming up new ideas spontaneously

What is the role of human oversight in AI systems?

A • To provide data for AI training

B • To ensure the AI operates within ethical boundaries and to evaluate its decisions

C • To make AI systems work faster

D • Human oversight is not necessary for AI systems

Is AI's ability to learn similar to how humans learn? Why or why not?

A • Yes, AI learns from experience just like humans

B • No, AI learns from large datasets and specific algorithms, unlike human learning

C • AI doesn't actually 'learn'; it just follows programmed instructions

D • AI learns in the same way as children do

True or False: AI systems are always 100% accurate

A • True

B • False

Give an example of a problem that AI might struggle to solve?

A • Playing chess at a high level.

B • Translating languages with high accuracy

C • Understanding and replicating human empathy

D • Sorting emails into spam and non-spam categories

What is the difference between narrow AI and general AI?

A • Narrow AI is designed for specific tasks, while general AI has human-like intelligence and can perform any intellectual task.

B • Narrow AI is less intelligent

C • General AI is just a theory and does not exist yet

D • There is no difference; they are just different terms for the same thing

How does AI contribute to advancements in healthcare?

A • By scheduling patient appointments
B • By providing virtual nursing assistants
C • By enhancing diagnostic procedures and personalized medicine
D • AI does not contribute to healthcaree

What are some ways to address bias in AI systems?

A • Use more diverse datasets
B • Ignore the problem as it does not affect AI performance
C • Program the AI to not make biased decisions
D • Utilize algorithmic audits and fairness metrics

Where do you see AI having the most significant impact in the next decade?

A • In replacing all jobs, leading to massive unemployment
B • In enhancing creative fields such as music and art
C • In optimizing supply chains and logistics
D • AI will not have a significant impact

Find the correction p122

2

AI to augment yourself and your business

Chapter 6
Launching and Scaling Your Startup - A Guided Framework

Embarking on the startup journey is an exhilarating challenge that requires more than just a groundbreaking idea. It's a path that demands courage, strategic planning, and a deep understanding of the market landscape. Drawing upon the wisdom shared by Paul Graham, here are essential steps and considerations for anyone ready to start their entrepreneurial venture.

1. **Start with a Problem:** Identify a problem that you are passionate about solving. The most successful startups begin with a genuine need, providing solutions that address real-world issues. Your connection to the problem will fuel your persistence and creativity.

2. **Build a Great Team:** Behind every successful startup is a dynamic team. Co-founders should complement each other's skills and share a common vision for the company. Collaboration, mutual respect, and shared commitment form the backbone of any thriving venture.

3. **Focus on the Product:** In the initial stages, your primary focus should be on developing a product or service that offers tangible value to your users. Prioritize simplicity and user experience, ensuring that your solution effectively solves the identified problem.

4. **Seek Feedback Early and Often:** Engage with potential users as early as possible. Real-world feedback is invaluable, helping you refine your product and business model. Be open to criticism and ready to iterate based on user insights.

5. **Understand Your Market:** A deep understanding of your target market is crucial. Research your competitors, understand your potential customers, and identify a clear value proposition. Your startup should not only fill a gap in the market but also stand out among existing solutions.

6. **Develop a Flexible Business Model:** Your initial business model may evolve as you learn more about your market and customers. Stay flexible and be prepared to pivot if necessary. The ability to adapt to feedback and changing market dynamics is a key strength.

(7) Secure Funding Wisely: While securing funding is a significant milestone, it's essential to approach it strategically. Consider the timing, amount, and source of funding carefully, ensuring it aligns with your growth plans without diluting your vision.

(8) Embrace the Startup Mindset: Starting a startup is a marathon, not a sprint. It requires resilience, adaptability, and a willingness to face uncertainty. Embrace challenges as opportunities for growth and learning.

(9) Focus on Growth: Once your product or service is in the market, prioritize growth. Experiment with different strategies to acquire users and scale your business. Sustainable growth is often the best indicator of product-market fit.

(10) Maintain Your Vision: Amid the ups and downs of the startup journey, it's crucial to keep your overarching vision in focus. Stay true to your mission, and let it guide your decisions and strategies as you navigate the complex landscape of entrepreneurship.

Starting a startup is an adventure. By following these steps, entrepreneurs can lay a strong foundation for their venture, poised for growth and impact in their chosen markets. Remember, the journey of a startup is as much about the process of discovery and learning as it is about achieving success.

8 Lessons Entrepreneurs Learn Through Experience

Many of these insights, gained through firsthand experience, shape the entrepreneur's path and are crucial for the success and growth of their ventures.

1. **Persistence Is Key:** One of the most critical realizations that entrepreneurs come to understand is the sheer importance of persistence. The path to success is often littered with obstacles, and it's the continuous effort, despite challenges, that separates successful ventures from those that falter.

2. **The Importance of Real User Feedback:** Entrepreneurs quickly learn that their initial idea or product may not perfectly align with market needs. Engaging directly with users to gather feedback becomes an invaluable practice, guiding significant pivots or minor adjustments that significantly enhance the product-market fit.

3. **The Art of Selling:** Whether it's pitching to investors or convincing your first customers, selling is an art that entrepreneurs must master. The realization that a great idea alone isn't enough without the ability to sell it effectively is a game-changer for many startups.

4. **Focus on Quality and Simplicity:** In the quest to innovate, entrepreneurs learn the hard lesson that complexity doesn't equate to value. A simple, well-executed solution often trumps a complex one, emphasizing the importance of focusing on core functionality and quality.

5. **The Value of a Committed Team:** Building a business is not a solo endeavor. Entrepreneurs learn the hard way that the right team can make or break their startup. The importance of surrounding oneself with individuals who share the vision and dedication to the project is paramount.

6. **Financial Prudence:** Managing cash flow effectively is a lesson often learned through struggle. Entrepreneurs find out the hard way that every dollar counts and that financial prudence can extend their runway significantly, giving them more time to achieve their goals.

7 **Adaptability:** The entrepreneurial journey is unpredictable, and the ability to adapt to changing circumstances is a lesson learned through experience. Those who can pivot in response to market feedback or unforeseen challenges are more likely to succeed.

8 **The Role of Luck:** Finally, entrepreneurs come to appreciate the role of luck in their success. While hard work, strategy, and perseverance are crucial, being in the right place at the right time can also play a significant role.

These lessons, learned through the trials and tribulations of entrepreneurship, are not merely hurdles but stepping stones to building a resilient, adaptable, and successful business. As the role of the entrepreneur evolves, these insights become the foundation upon which future strategies and innovations are built

Why Startups Fail: A Data-Driven Insight

The journey of a startup is fraught with potential pitfalls, and data reveals a sobering narrative of high failure rates and common challenges. As we venture into understanding why startups falter, let's consider the stark statistics: by the end of the first year, 20% of new businesses have already failed, a figure that climbs to 50% by the end of the fifth year, and by the tenth year, 70% of startups have closed their doors.

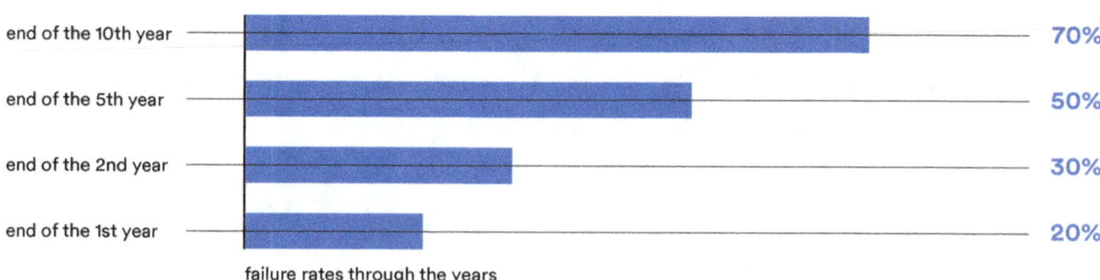

Failure Rates Of All New Businesses

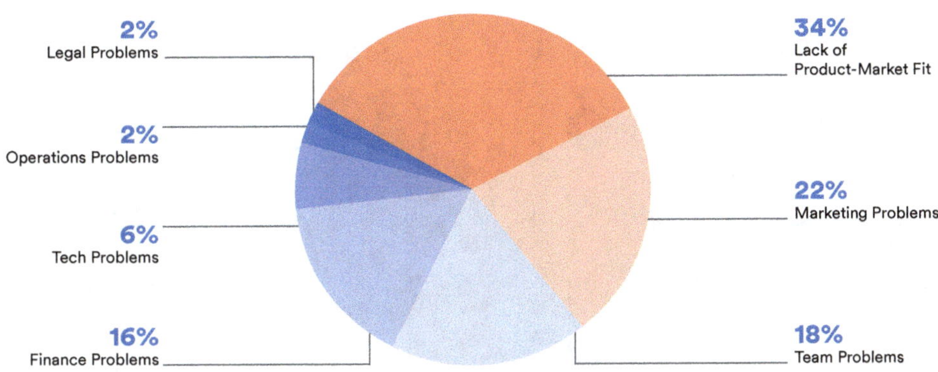

Analyzing the reasons behind these failures uncovers several key areas where startups commonly stumble. The lack of product-market fit emerges as the primary culprit, accounting for 34% of failures. This highlights the crucial need for startups to ensure that their product genuinely addresses the needs and desires of the market.

Marketing problems are another significant challenge, representing 22% of startup failures. This statistic underscores the importance of a robust go-to-market strategy and the ability to connect with customers effectively.

Team problems contribute to 18% of failures, emphasizing that the right mix of skills, experience, and team dynamics is vital for success.

Financial problems are not far behind, with 16% of startups failing due to cash flow issues, underscoring the importance of financial prudence and management.

Technology issues, legal challenges, and operational difficulties collectively account for 10% of startup failures, indicating that while these areas are critical, the human-centric aspects of a startup such as market fit, team dynamics, and marketing strategies are even more pivotal.

Lastly, the failure rate has profound implications for startup investors. While a portfolio may see many failures, it is often the few successful startups, including the rare unicorn, that can more than compensate for the losses.

Failure Rate Implications For Startup Investors

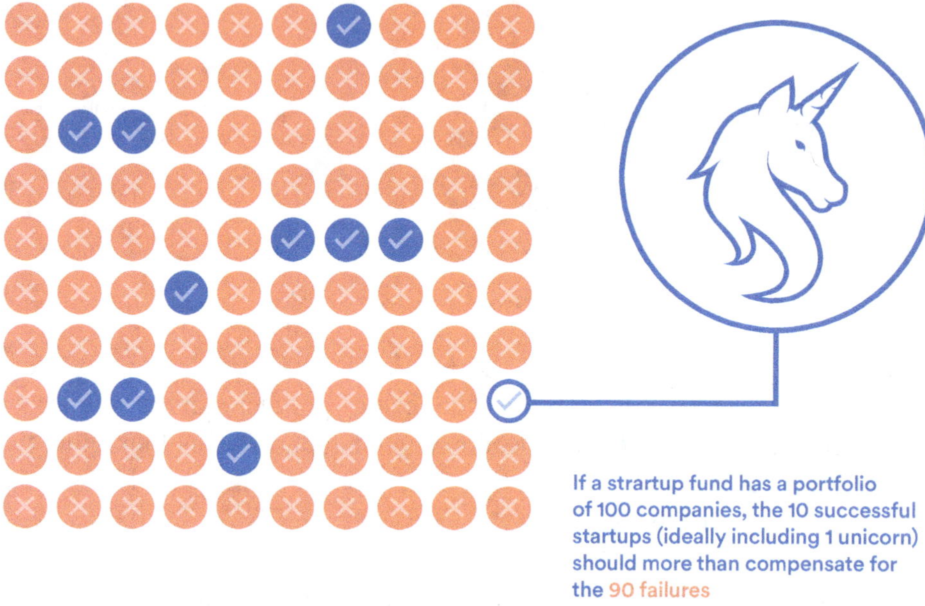

The $1,000 billion question is... How can we leverage AI to limit the risk of failure and make the path to success as safe as possible?

You'll become a crisis management sniper

Scaling a startup is akin to ascending a staircase with its own unique set of plateaus; each level demands stabilization before moving upward. XAnge's analysis sheds light on the inevitable growth crises that startups encounter during this climb. Entrepreneurs must recognize that these challenges are not just hurdles but also opportunities for strengthening their business's core. The journey of scaling is standardized yet unforgiving, with each startup facing its own battles against common crises. It's essential to understand that experiencing a growth crisis is a natural, and even beneficial, part of the scaling process. Rather than turning a blind eye to the looming difficulties, addressing them head-on is crucial. Acknowledgment and proactive management of these challenges are what differentiate thriving companies from those that falter. It's about embracing resilience and perseverance, not just within the entrepreneur but across the entire organization, to transform these crises into valuable lessons for sustainable growth.

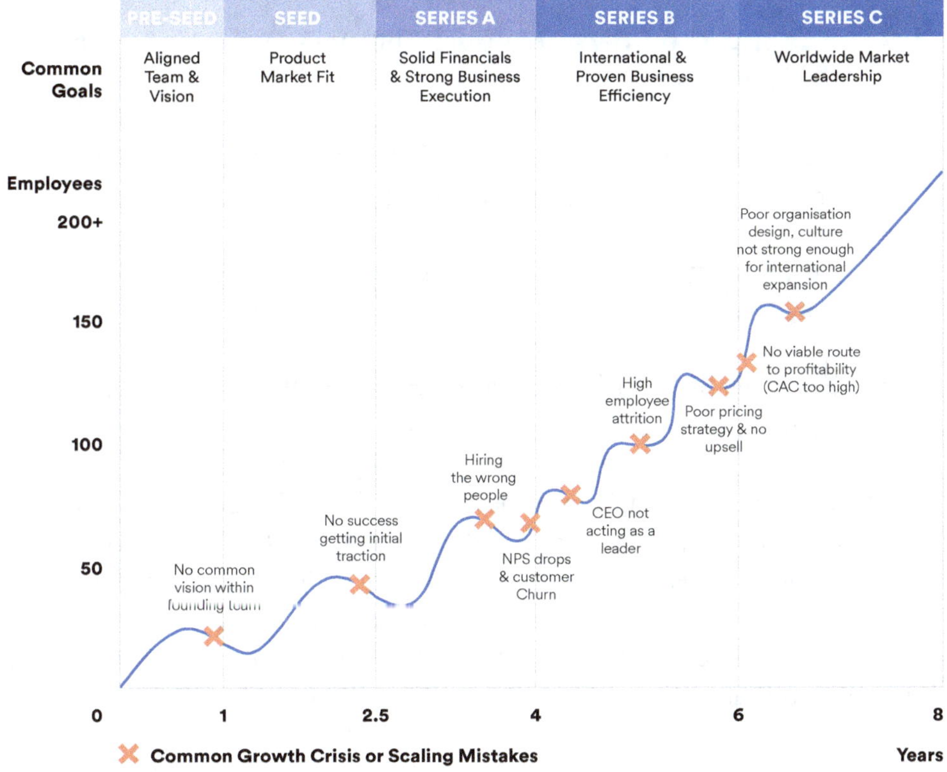

As we close this chapter on launching and scaling your startup, we've traversed the landscape of rapid growth, familiarized ourselves with the common crises that lie in wait, and gleaned insights from both the meteoric rise of unicorns and the pitfalls that have ensnared others. A pivotal revelation stands before us: the entrepreneur, the visionary at the helm, often becomes the inadvertent choke point of the organization. The ability to scale oneself and the organization is a skill not inherent, but one that must be consciously developed.

Armed with this knowledge, we pivot to the promise of artificial intelligence as an indispensable ally in the chapters ahead. AI holds the power to amplify your execution capabilities, providing what we may term an 'unfair advantage' over the competition. We will delve into the transformative influence of AI across four fundamental pillars:

1. **Scaling the Entrepreneur:** Enhancing your leadership and decision-making capacity.

2. **Securing Product-Market Fit:** Leveraging AI for iterative product development and achieving market resonance.

3. **Building a Successful Team:** Utilizing AI for talent acquisition, team dynamics, and operational efficiency

4. **Solving Marketing Challenges:** Applying AI to refine marketing strategies and drive growth.

As we move forward, let us not just anticipate the transformative potential of AI but actively engage with it to reshape the very fabric of our entrepreneurial endeavors. The journey is arduous, but the rewards are commensurate with the courage to embark upon it. Let's step into the future, where AI does not just support but accelerates our vision, molding startups into titans of industry.

Chapter 7
The evolving role of the entrepreneur

What's my role?

Navigating the turbulent waters of startup leadership, an entrepreneur wears many hats, but fundamentally, their role distills down to three core jobs. Inspired by the wisdom imparted by Paul Graham, Y Combinator's co-founder and Harvard University lecturer, these roles form the bedrock of entrepreneurial success

1 The Maker: Crafting a Product Users Love

One of the most critical realizations that entrepreneurs come to understand is the sheer importance of persistence. The path to success is often littered with obstacles, and it's the continuous effort, despite challenges, that separates successful ventures from those that falter.

2 The Manager: Building a Company to Maximize Opportunity

Once you've captured the hearts of your users, it's time to scale. Your role evolves into that of a manager. This means putting systems in place, hiring the right people, and setting the vision for growth. You'll focus on culture, operational efficiency, and assembling a team that can carry your vision forward.

③ The Messenger: Telling Your Story

Finally, as an entrepreneur, you're also the chief storyteller. Whether it's to investors, customers, or your own team, your job is to communicate the core message of your startup with clarity and passion. This means crafting narratives that connect emotionally and rationalize logically, spreading the word about why what you're doing matters.

Balancing these roles isn't easy, and where you should spend your time will shift as your startup grows. In the beginning, expect to be deeply involved in product development. As your startup matures, delegate to trust your team with the day-to-day, so you can focus on strategic growth and communicating your vision to the world.

Remember, being an entrepreneur is a dynamic role that changes with your company's lifecycle. The key is to adapt, anticipate, and always be ready for the next hat that you'll need to wear.

To progress along this ladder, you need to become an ace delegator. Here are a few prompts, suggested by the brilliant Jodie Cook Founder of Coachvox AI, that you can use to get AI to help you delegate:

① Feel the pain of not delegating

«Given my business, [describe your business], and my current role as [describe your role], I'm aiming towards [describe a big goal] as my ultimate business goal. Currently, I'm handling tasks such as [tasks you suspect are below your potential] on my own, without delegating. Could you illustrate a bleak and discouraging future scenario for both my business and personal life if I continue this way? I'm looking for a 2-3 paragraph narrative that starkly outlines the consequences of failing to delegate, including the impact on my business growth, personal well-being, and overall life satisfaction. This narrative should serve as a wake-up call, compelling me to start delegating effectively.»

② Understand your superpowers

«Significant wins in my entrepreneurial journey include: [describe a recent win], [describe another win], and [describe a third win]. These achievements have shaped the trajectory of my business and my personal development. Based on these successes, could you suggest what my top 3 superpowers might be? These superpowers are skills or attributes I possess that have consistently contributed to my wins and set me apart from others. After your initial suggestions, I'll agree or disagree with each, and we can refine the list until we identify my definitive top 3 superpowers. This understanding will help me leverage these strengths in every aspect of my work, aiming to maximize my impact and outpace competition.»

③ Decide what to delegate

I've identified my superpowers with your help, and now I need to focus on the flip side: tasks that don't play to my strengths, things I find tedious, or tasks that consume too much of my time without adding significant value. Some of these tasks include [a task you don't enjoy], [a task that takes too long], and [a task you're not great at]. Based on these, and including the reverse of my strengths mentioned earlier, could you suggest 10 tasks that I should consider delegating to others? Organize these tasks into a three-column table, with the first column being the number of each process, the second containing the title of the process to delegate, and the third suggesting an action plan for each delegation. The list should be ordered by priority, allowing me to address the most critical or time-consuming tasks first and proceed in a way that methodically frees up my schedule.»

④ Create your boundaries:

«I'm refining my delegation process to empower my team more effectively. To guide this, I need to create 'if this, then that' rules for training people and setting boundaries to avoid micromanagement. Key scenarios include feeling a lack of control and how to hand over tasks properly. Help me establish 7 succinct, actionable guidelines, such as: 'If [I feel a lack of control], then [I will assess its validity before acting],' and 'Before [I delegate a task], I will [ensure training and require an SOP].' These rules will be based on my business [type/description], my role as [your role], and aiming towards [your ultimate goal].»

5 Incorporate a feedback loop

«I've recently handed off [specific task/project] to [team member/ department]. While I believe in the capabilities of my team, I'm concerned about [describe specific concerns, such as maintaining quality, adhering to timelines, or ensuring the task aligns with broader business objectives]. To address these concerns, keep improving, and elevate our standards, I'm seeking your guidance on creating effective feedback loops for this particular delegation. Can you help me design a detailed, step-by-step guide on what to measure, when and how to communicate feedback, and strategies for ongoing improvement of the process? This guide should not only help in addressing my current concerns but also set a foundation for continuous elevation of performance standards across my team.»

Generative AI's Skills Card

As we move ahead, let's delve deeper into the capabilities of our new team member, Generative AI, by mapping out its skills card. This skills card will shed light on its strengths, weaknesses, and tasks best suited for.

Let's start with the **strengths**. AI excels in areas such as:

1 Pattern Recognition and Prediction: AIs can identify patterns and trends in vast datasets faster and more accurately than any human could. For example, an AI can predict a customer's future purchases based on past behavior, improving the effectiveness of marketing efforts.

2 Repetitive Task Automation: AI can automate routine, repetitive tasks, freeing up human workers for more complex duties.

Think of customer service chatbots that handle common queries, allowing human agents to tackle more challenging customer issues.

3 Generating New Content: Generative AI can create new content, from writing articles to designing graphics, based on the patterns it's learned. For example, AI tools like GPT-4 can generate human-like text, aiding content creation in various fields.

However, AI isn't without its **weaknesses**:

1 Lack of Emotional Intelligence: While AI can analyze data, it can't understand or express human emotions. For instance, an AI customer service agent can't empathize with a frustrated customer in the same way a human can.

2 Limited Creativity: AI can generate content based on existing patterns but can't truly innovate or think outside the box. It's humans who excel in generating novel ideas and solutions.

3 Ethical and Privacy Concerns: The use of AI, particularly in data analysis, raises ethical issues around privacy and data usage. These concerns need to be managed carefully to maintain trust.

Understanding these strengths and weaknesses is crucial for knowing where Generative AI fits into our teams and how to best work together. In the coming pages, we'll delve further into the specific tasks susceptible to automation and how they might affect different professions. Let's continue unraveling this complex but fascinating subject together.

Keeping up with the rapid evolution of AI

In the fast-evolving landscape of AI, staying updated is not just a matter of competitive advantage—it's essential for survival. Here's how you can keep pace:

Establish a Learning Routine:

Dedicate a minimum of two hours each week exclusively to exploring AI innovations. This time should be spent experimenting with new tools and platforms that could enhance your business processes. Maintain an "AI toolkit" folder on your smartphone or computer where you can readily access and test various AI applications such as Perplexity, Midjourney, and Runway. This hands-on approach will deepen your understanding of AI capabilities and how they can be harnessed to accelerate your execution.

Curate Your Information Sources:

Subscribe to leading AI-focused newsletters like Import AI and AI Weekly to receive curated content on the latest developments in the field. These resources condense complex information into digestible insights, keeping you informed without overwhelming you. Additionally, following AI innovators and thought leaders on social media platforms such as Instagram, with accounts like Evolving AI, can offer visual and interactive ways to learn about AI trends and applications.

Invest in Your AI Knowledge:

Don't shy away from spending on AI tools. Services like ChatGPT, HeyGen, and others often have features behind paywalls that could be immensely beneficial for your business. By investing in these tools, you not only get firsthand experience with cutting-edge technology but also support the ecosystem that continues to drive AI forward. Think of these expenses as investments in your company's future and your personal development as an entrepreneur who understands and leverages AI.

Remember, integrating AI into your business is not a one-time event but an ongoing process of learning, experimenting, and adapting.

Chapter 8
AI & Product Development

AI is transforming product development, empowering creators to design products that truly resonate with users. It levels the playing field, allowing anyone with an idea to bring it to life, and personalizes the user experience by enabling products to adapt based on feedback. This section will explore AI's impact on reaching product-market fit, enhancing market research, and the synergy between AI and NoCode tools, showcasing AI as a catalyst for innovation in the digital marketplace.

Leveraging AI for Precision-Driven Market Research

In the realm of product development, understanding your market is half the battle won. AI has taken this understanding to new heights, offering tools that not only streamline the process but also provide deep, actionable insights. Here are practical, AI-powered solutions and how they're reshaping market research.

AI-Powered Consumer Insights: Brandwatch and Crimson Hexagon

Forget traditional surveys; platforms like Brandwatch and Crimson Hexagon use AI to analyze social media chatter, offering real-time insights into consumer sentiment and emerging trends. For example, a startup in the sustainable clothing space could use these tools to monitor discussions around sustainability, identifying niches or specific concerns among potential customers, such as interest in zero-waste packaging.

Predictive Analytics: GPT-4 and TensorFlow

Tools like OpenAI's GPT-4 and Google's TensorFlow are revolutionizing predictive analytics, enabling businesses to forecast trends and consumer behavior with unprecedented accuracy. Netflix, for instance, leverages predictive models to tailor content recommendations, but smaller companies can also use these tools to anticipate market demands, optimizing their product offerings accordingly.

Segmentation and Targeting: HubSpot and Marketo

With AI, segmentation isn't just about demographics but nuanced behaviors and preferences. Platforms like HubSpot and Marketo utilize AI to segment audiences based on their online behavior and engagement, allowing for highly targeted marketing campaigns. A beauty brand could use these tools to identify and target individuals showing interest in cruelty-free products, even if they haven't explicitly searched for them.

Competitive Analysis: Semrush and Ahrefs

Understanding your competition is crucial, and AI tools like Semrush and Ahrefs provide a wealth of data on competitors' online strategies. These tools can track everything from SEO rankings to social media engagement, offering insights on how to adjust your strategy. An e-commerce business could use these platforms to monitor competitors' pricing strategies and promotional campaigns, adapting in real time to maintain a competitive edge.

Voice of the Customer: Chattermill and Qualtrics

AI-driven platforms like Chattermill and Qualtrics analyze customer feedback across various channels, translating unstructured data into actionable insights. This capability allows companies to refine their products based on direct customer input, ensuring they meet market needs more effectively.

AI's Role in Achieving Product-Market Fit

Product-market fit occurs when a product satisfies a strong market demand. It's a crucial milestone for startups, indicating that their product has been validated by the market and has a sustainable, scalable customer base.

Consider the analogy of selling lottery numbers. If you're selling next week's winning lottery numbers, you're offering something of immense value that meets a significant demand—everyone wants to win the lottery, and if you can genuinely predict those numbers, your product (the winning numbers) perfectly fits the market's desire. This scenario exemplifies excellent product-market fit: the product directly addresses a strong, existing demand.

On the other hand, trying to sell last week's winning lottery numbers is a clear case of missing the product-market fit. Despite the product (winning numbers) being valuable in a different context, it no longer meets any demand since the lottery has passed. Nobody needs or wants this information anymore, highlighting a complete disconnect between the product and the market needs.

Product-market fit (PMF) encompasses three critical elements: desirability, feasibility, and viability. These components are developed gradually as you refine your product offering

Reflecting on the lottery ticket analogy, achieving a strong PMF is characterized by:

- Minimal to No Discounts: This indicates that the product is highly desired at its current price point, demonstrating its value to customers.

- Scalable Sales Team: The product sells itself to a large extent, eliminating the need for a team of superstar salespeople.

- High Repeatability: Customers are satisfied and likely to seek the product repeatedly, signifying enduring appeal and sustained demand.

Conversely, signs of a weak PMF include:

- Significant Discounts. Required to make the product appealing, suggesting it lacks inherent value or does not meet a significant need.

- Costly Sales Efforts: A sales team that struggles to close deals or must be highly skilled and expensive to be effective, indicating the product does not naturally fit market demands.

- Low Repeatability: Customers do not return for repeat purchases, implying that the product fails to meet expectations or sustain interest over time.

In essence, a good PMF means your product is inherently desirable, operationally feasible, and economically viable, leading to a self-sustaining cycle of demand, sales, and growth. A lack of PMF, however, reflects a disconnect between the product and the market's needs, resulting in unsustainable sales practices and poor customer retention.

The Process Towards PMF

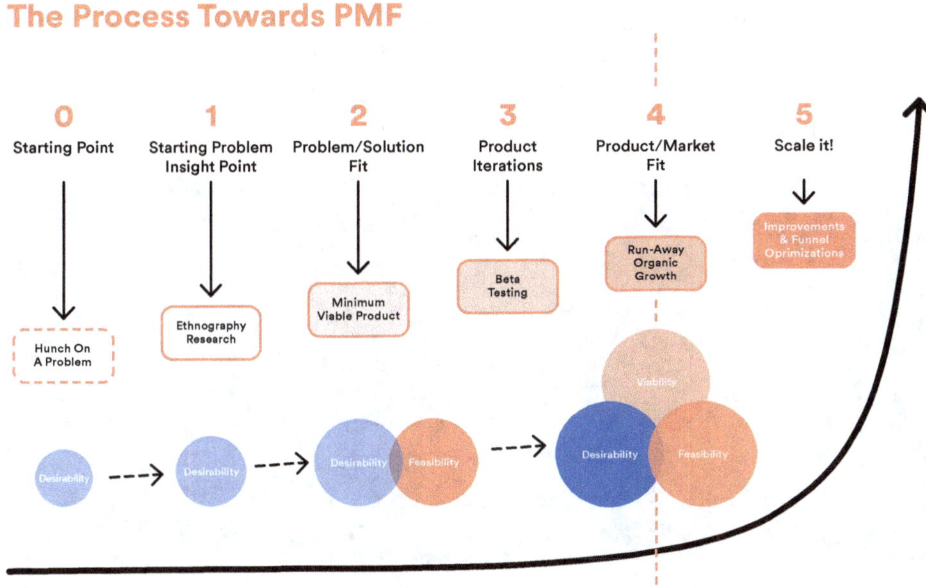

In the journey to achieving product-market fit, AI tools have emerged as powerful allies, enabling entrepreneurs to streamline the process from ideation to validation and optimization. Here's how AI can make a significant difference:

1 Rapid Prototyping and Validation

Tools: Bubble, Softr, and Galileo AI.

The early stages of a startup are all about speed and agility. Tools like Bubble and Softr allow entrepreneurs to turn ideas into functional prototypes without deep technical skills, leveraging a no-code approach. This democratization of development means you can go from concept to prototype swiftly, testing your ideas in the real world sooner.

Galileo AI stands out by transforming textual descriptions into design prototypes. Imagine sketching out your product's concept in words and having a visual prototype ready in just hours. This capability not only accelerates the prototyping phase but also opens up opportunities for rapid A/B testing and user feedback collection, crucial for refining your value proposition.

To give you a concrete illustration, I set myself the task of translating an idea into a product thanks to AI, with 0 technical or design skills. Children are fans of cartoon heroes. So I came up with an app that lets children chat, in complete safety, with an AI clone of their favorite character. The child can have a facetime, a written conversation or a phone call with his or her heroes. I used Galileo to translate my idea into an app, and here are some of the results obtained in 15 minutes:

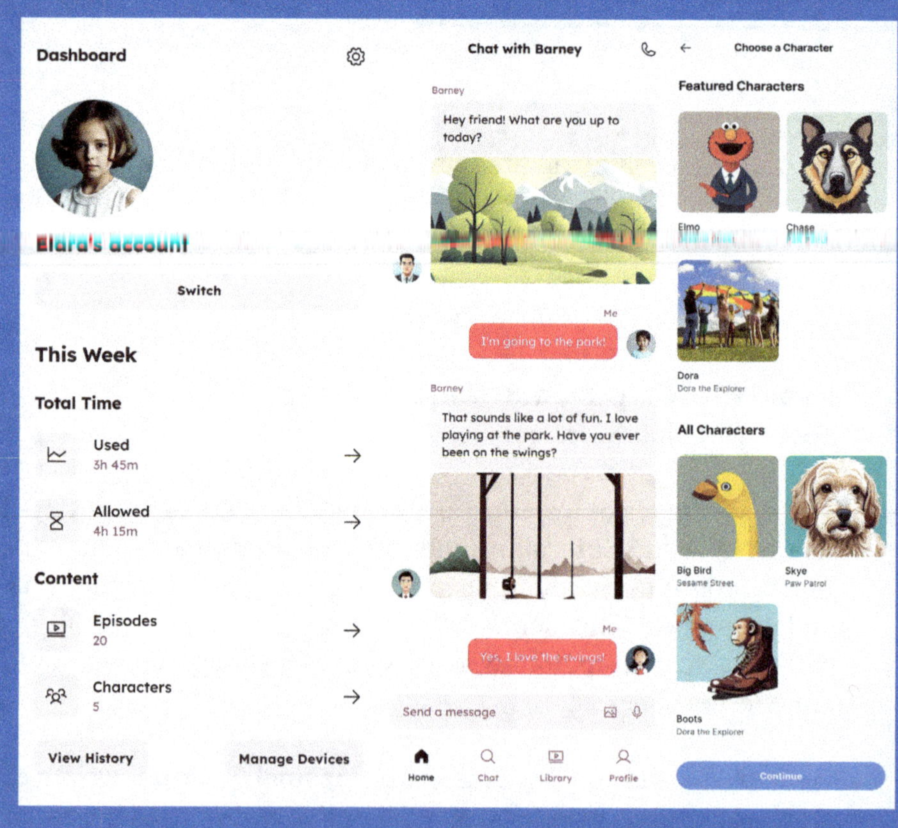

② Data-Driven Iterations

Tools: Mixpanel and Amplitude

Once your MVP (Minimum Viable Product) is in users' hands, the next step is to iterate based on real user data. Mixpanel and Amplitude shine here, offering deep insights into how users interact with your product. By analyzing user behavior, startups can identify features that resonate with their audience and areas that require improvement. This data-driven approach ensures that each iteration brings you closer to a product that truly meets market needs.

③ Predictive Analytics for Market Trends

Tools: Google Trends and TrendKite

Understanding and anticipating market trends is crucial for achieving product-market fit. Google Trends offers a straightforward, accessible way to gauge interest in certain topics or products over time, helping you align your offerings with emerging demands. TrendKite takes it a step further by providing AI-powered media monitoring, enabling startups to track how their industry is evolving and how their brand is perceived. This insight is invaluable for positioning your product effectively and staying ahead of market shifts.

Incorporating AI tools into the product development process not only accelerates the journey to product-market fit but also provides a more nuanced understanding of the market and user needs. By leveraging these technologies, startups can make informed decisions, iterate rapidly, and ultimately deliver products that truly resonate with their target audience.

Chapter 9

People - Building a successful team thanks to AI

Transitioning from the role of a Maker—what Paul Graham likes to call the Chief Doer Officer—to that of a Manager is a pivotal shift in the entrepreneurial journey. This transformation hinges not just on your ability to execute but on your capacity to assemble and nurture the right team. The insights I'm about to share are culled from a blend of personal trials and triumphs, insightful interviews with successful entrepreneurs (some of whom have exited their ventures for up to $3.5 billion), a thorough review of existing literature, and my own research conducted at Harvard University alongside leading figures in the field.

In the quest to build a high-performing team, four critical activities emerge as indispensable:

1. continuously adapting your organization,

2. identifying and attracting the best talent,

3. maintaining talent density, and

4. crafting effective teams.

Each of these activities is challenging, requiring not just intuition and determination but a nuanced understanding of both human dynamics and the operational needs of your business.

Remarkably, artificial intelligence (AI) offers potent tools that can significantly ease these challenges. AI's capabilities, from streamlining recruitment processes to enhancing team dynamics and decision-making, are transforming how we think about building and managing teams. In this chapter, we'll explore step by step how AI can be leveraged to master these four critical activities, facilitating a smoother transition for entrepreneurs stepping into their managerial roles.

Continuously adapting your organization

Designing the optimal organization for success is more art than science, blending strategic foresight with the adaptability to navigate an ever-changing business landscape. It's a crucial endeavor, underscored by striking statistics: organizations with mature organizational designs are 30 times more likely to adapt effectively to change, 5.3 times more likely to be considered great places to work, and 2.3 times more likely to exceed financial targets. Despite these compelling figures, a mere 11% of organizations reach high maturity in organizational design, with over 70% having maintained their current structures for five years or more.

This process remains largely manual and specific to each company, yet certain principles and AI tools can guide this crucial task.

When is the right time? In reality, the sooner you build the right organization, the more you reduce the risk of recruitment errors. Distributing tasks in the right way within your organization contributes to the sustainability of your business (meaning you'll be recruiting the right profiles for your strategy, at the right price).

Organizational Stages of Development

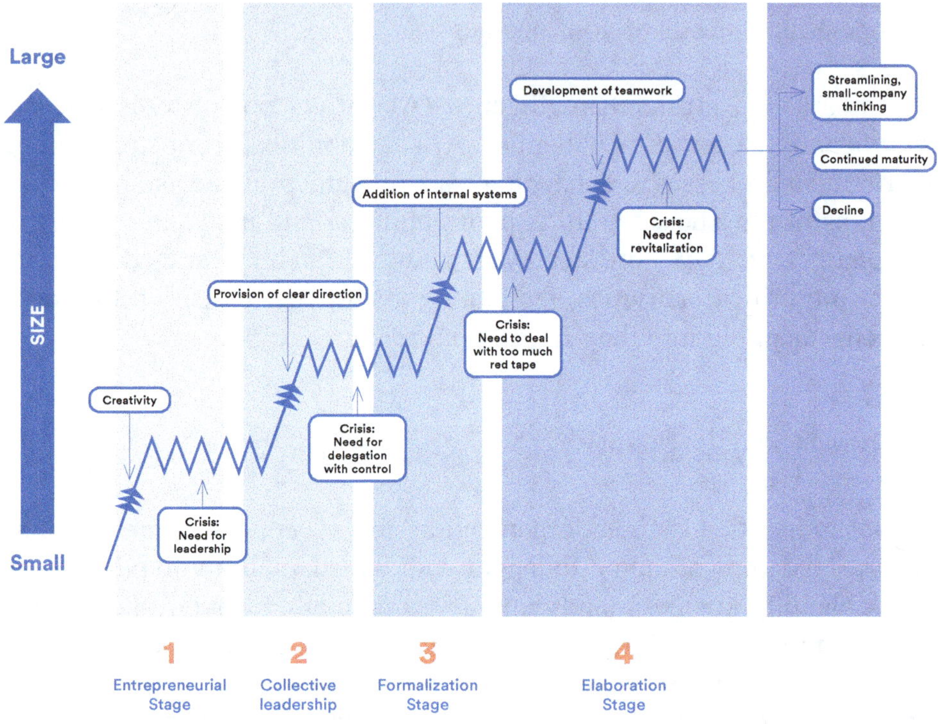

Designing the perfect organization is a dynamic and ongoing process that requires thoughtful analysis, creativity, and a willingness to adapt. Here's a streamlined five-step methodology to guide you through designing or re-evaluating your organizational structure:

1 Assess Organizational Goals and Strategy

Begin by clearly defining your organization's long-term goals and the strategy you plan to employ to achieve them. This foundational step ensures that the organizational design aligns with the overarching vision and mission. Consider the market you operate in, your value proposition, and how you differentiate yourself from competitors.

2 **Evaluate Current Organizational Performance**
Conduct a comprehensive assessment of your current organizational structure to identify strengths, weaknesses, opportunities, and threats (SWOT analysis). Utilize both qualitative and quantitative data to evaluate how well the current design supports operational efficiency, employee satisfaction, and goal achievement. Tools like employee surveys, performance metrics, and workflow analysis can provide invaluable insights during this phase.

3 **Identify Key Functions and Roles**
Based on your strategic objectives and performance evaluation, outline the essential functions that your organization needs to excel in to achieve its goals. This step involves mapping out key roles and responsibilities, ensuring clarity in what each part of the organization is accountable for. Consider emerging needs and potential areas of innovation that could require new roles or a realignment of existing ones.

4 **Leverage AI for Data-Driven Insights**
Integrate AI tools and data analytics to gain deeper insights into optimal organizational structures within your industry. AI can help benchmark against competitors, suggest efficient team sizes, and recommend skill sets needed for various roles based on current market trends. For example, AI-driven platforms can provide valuable data on optimal ratios for customer support staff to customers in a SaaS company or suggest sales quotas based on industry averages and historical performance data.

PROMPT

"Acting as an HR expert, you design the organization of the company operating in [market]. What are the relevant benchmark ratios that allow me to forecaster [role]?"

Implement, Monitor, and Adapt

With a clear design in place, begin implementing changes, starting with the most critical areas identified in your evaluation. Communication is key during this phase; ensure that all stakeholders understand the rationale behind changes and their roles within the new structure. Establish metrics to monitor the impact of these changes on organizational performance and employee satisfaction. Be prepared to adapt the structure based on feedback and evolving business needs, embracing a philosophy of continuous improvement.

One of the questions you'll ask yourself as you grow: when to recruit? Perhaps investors will have asked you for an excel forecast of your projected workforce. Just one rule to remember: don't recruit just because your excel spreadsheet tells you to. Otherwise you'll be creating a cash incinerator. You need to add a resource when you can integrate it and make it contribute.

It's not an easy exercise, but you can take inspiration from these four structurally different models:

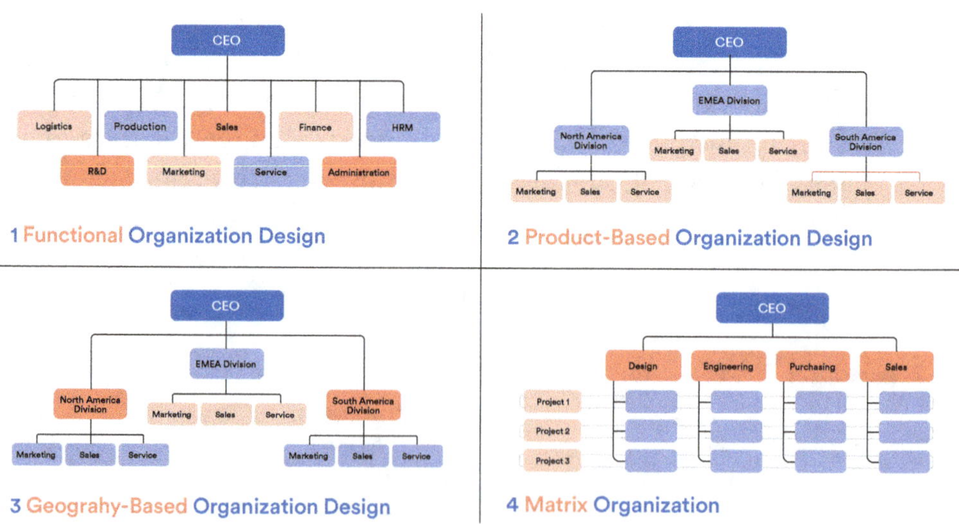

1 Functional Organization Design

2 Product-Based Organization Design

3 Geograhy-Based Organization Design

4 Matrix Organization

The image you've uploaded appears to show four types of organizational structures. Here's an explanation of each one based on the context of organizational design:

1 Functional Organizational Design

This type of structure groups employees based on their function or role within the company. Common departments in a functional structure include Logistics, Production, Sales, Finance, Human Resources Management (HRM), Research & Development (R&D), Marketing, Service, and Administration. This design facilitates specialization in tasks and centralizes expertise, but it can create silos within an organization, potentially leading to a lack of communication between departments.

Advantages
a. Specialization: Employees develop deep expertise in their function.
b. Efficiency: High efficiency in operations due to standardized processes.
c. Clarity: Clear career paths within specialized functions.

Disadvantages
a. Silos: Can lead to a lack of communication between departments.
b. Inflexibility: Responds slowly to changes in the market or customer needs.
c. Internal focus: Can lead to a narrow focus on departmental goals over the company's overall objectives.

2 Product-Based Organizational Design

In a product-based structure, the organization is divided into smaller, self-contained units responsible for a particular product line. Each product line, such as Electronics, Home Furnishing, or Foods, has its own dedicated Marketing, Sales, and Service departments. This structure allows teams to focus on their product's specific needs and market, fostering a quicker response to product-related challenges and customer demands.

Advantages

a. Focus: Teams are highly focused on the product and its performance.
b. Agility: Can respond rapidly to product-specific market changes.
c. Accountability: Clear responsibility for product success.

Disadvantages

a. Duplication: Potential for duplication of resources and efforts across products.
b. Conflict: Can create conflict over resource allocation among product lines.
c. Complexity: More complex coordination as the number of products increases.

3 Geography-Based Organizational Design

Geographic structuring is used by organizations that operate in different regions or countries. It's similar to the product-based structure but organized by location. For instance, there might be divisions for North America, EMEA (Europe, Middle East, and Africa), and South America. Each division would have its Marketing, Sales, and Service teams tailored to the specific needs and characteristics of the local market.

Advantages

a. Localization: Tailored strategies for local markets and cultures.
b. Responsiveness: Quick response to local trends and customer needs.
c. Autonomy: Local divisions have some autonomy to make decisions that best fit their market

Disadvantages

a. Fragmentation: Risk of inconsistent company-wide strategy

and culture.
b. Coordination: Difficulty in coordinating efforts across different geographical divisions.
c. Complexity: Management of diverse market demands can be complex and resource-intensive.

4 Matrix Organization

A matrix organization is a hybrid structure combining aspects of both functional and product-based designs. Employees report to both a functional manager and a product or project manager. This type of design aims to leverage the benefits of both functional expertise and product-specific focus. For example, individuals from the Design, Engineering, Purchasing, and Sales departments might be assigned to Project 1, Project 2, or Project 3, and they must navigate the demands of both their departmental and project roles.

Advantages
a. Flexibility: Ability to allocate resources to projects as needed.
b. Dynamic teams: Employees can work across different functions and projects.
c. Knowledge sharing: Enhances communication and knowledge sharing between functions.

Disadvantages
a. Power struggle: Potential for conflict between functional and project managers.
b. Complexity: Increased complexity in management and communications.
c. Overhead: Can lead to increased overhead with more managers required.

The choice among these organizational structures typically depends on the company's size, strategy, complexity, and the markets it serves. The decision on which structure to adopt should align with the company's operational needs and strategic goals.

Identifying and attracting the best talent

The Art of Talent Sourcing

In the realm of high-stakes entrepreneurship, the acquisition of top-tier talent is not just an HR function—it's a strategic imperative. Here, we explore the art of talent acquisition, not through conventional means, but through strategic talent sourcing. This is where the chess game begins, and the players are none other than the best minds in the industry. I've made so many recruitment mistakes, I've been able to identify four (cumulative) approaches that help you source the right profiles.

1 Laying the Foundation: Crafting the Job Description
Before the search begins, there's a foundational task that sets the tone for all that follows: the creation of a clear, comprehensive job description. This document is more than a list of responsibilities; it's a map that guides the candidate to see themselves as part of your journey. To do this effectively, you need to engage in a deep dive into industry benchmarks, ensuring that the role is competitive and attractive. The job description should be a blend of precision and aspiration, outlining not just the skills required but also the impact the role is intended to have.

A job description should be designed to filter in the exceptional and filter out the incompatible. It should encompass the following:
   a. Core Responsibilities: A detailed, bullet-pointed list of the duties the role will entail.
   b. Expected Behaviors: A description of the behavioral attributes that align with your company's values and culture.
   c. Skillset Specifications: A breakdown of the technical and soft skills necessary for success in the role.

2 Cooptation: The Inside Job

Cooptation, or employee referral programs, should be the cornerstone of your sourcing strategy. It's akin to having an army of scouts; your own employees know the culture, the work ethic, and the drive needed to thrive in your company. When they refer someone, they are staking their own reputation on their referral's performance. This method of talent sourcing turns each employee into a stakeholder in the company's future, which is why many successful organizations reward successful referrals generously.

3 Word of Mouth: The Power of the Whisper Network

Word of mouth is the old soul of sourcing strategies, yet it remains potent. It's organic, it's authentic, and it speaks to the reputation of your company. In an age where company culture is as visible as its products, a good word from your current employees can be the beacon that attracts talent from afar. It's less about posting a job and hoping for the best, and more about creating an environment where the best want to be a part of what you're building.

4 Targeted Recruitment: The Sniper Approach

(my favorite sourcing strategy)

Imagine you had the opportunity to handpick your competitors' best players for your team. This is targeted recruitment—identifying the top 10 performers in your field and engaging them with the precision of a sniper. You don't wait for these talents to come to you; you go to them. But this approach isn't just about identifying; it's about closing them as you would a high-value client. This means understanding their motivations, their career aspirations, and presenting them with a narrative of how their ambitions align with the trajectory of your company.

In this part of the recruitment odyssey, your role transcends that of a mere employer—you become a visionary, selling the dream of what could be. You are not just offering a job; you are inviting them to embark on a career-defining journey.

In all these strategies, the common denominator is a paradigm shift from passive recruitment to active sourcing. It's about creating a magnetic pull that doesn't just draw candidates in, but also aligns them with the very heart of your organization's mission and culture. In the next section, we will explore how to refine this pull into a precise science using the best selection methodologies grounded in empirical evidence and data analytics.

The Art of Selection

When the goal is to secure top-tier talent, the methodology of the selection process becomes a linchpin for success. A profound insight emerges from a study by Harvard researchers: the difference between structured and unstructured interviews is not merely procedural but substantially impacts the odds of hiring a top performer. The study presents an array of selection tools, each quantified by a validity coefficient estimate, which represents the probability of hiring a high performer – a kind of efficacy rate for each method.

In the quest for the most effective hiring practice, structured interviews stand out, with a validity coefficient estimate of .71. This figure illuminates a compelling truth: by implementing a structured approach, an organization

Predictor	Validity coefficient estimante
General cognitive ability	.53 .48
Specific cognitive ability	.40–.50 .35–.50
Emotional intelligence	.28–.29
Psychomotor ability	.53 .40
Personality tests	.20–.30 .21–.37
Integrity tests (work performance)	.12–.15
Integrity tests (CWB)	.26–.32
Work samples	.44 .39
Situational judgment tests	.24–.38
Assessment centers	.38–.45 .28 .40
Biodata	.52 .37 .20–.46
Structured interviews	.71
Unstructured interviews	.20

has a 71% chance of hiring a top performer, which is more than threefold the effectiveness of unstructured interviews, clocking in at a mere. 20.

The structured interview, as implied by its name, is methodical and consistent. It involves a predetermined set of questions aimed at evaluating the critical competencies and skills pertinent to the job. This approach mitigates the risks of bias, ensures a level playing field for all candidates, and allows for a clear comparison of responses. The crux of the structured interview's superiority lies in its predictability and the quality of data it produces, which leads to more informed hiring decisions.

The Harvard study presents a clear case for embracing structured interviews as a cornerstone of the hiring process. By doing so, organizations can significantly improve their chances of hiring individuals who will excel in their roles. The method's robustness comes from its ability to systematically probe each candidate's suitability for the role's specific demands – both in terms of skill set and alignment with the company's culture and values.

To capitalize on the efficacy of structured interviews, organizations must:

1. Develop a comprehensive interview guide with questions aligned to key job competencies.

2. Train interviewers to conduct the interview and evaluate responses consistently.

3. Use a scoring system to objectively assess each candidate's responses.

4. Incorporate questions that allow candidates to demonstrate their problem-solving and critical-thinking skills.

In the broader picture of talent acquisition, this disciplined approach to interviews acts as a keystone, anchoring the hiring process in data-driven practices that maximize the probability of bringing onboard individuals who will not only fulfill their roles but thrive in them.

Based on this prompt, here's an example of how you might structure your interview guidelines for a Key Account Manager:

Structured Interview Guidelines for Key Account Manager Position

INTRODUCTION

- Welcome the candidate and explain the structure of the interview.
- Ensure the candidate is comfortable and understands that questions are designed to assess fit for the role.

Core Competency Questions

1. **Client Relationship Management:** «Describe a time when you had to build a relationship with a new key client. What strategies did you use, and what was the outcome?» Scoring Criteria: Evidence of strategic thinking, relationship-building skills, and successful outcomes.

2. **Strategic Sales Planning:** «Can you walk us through your process for developing a sales plan for a high-priority account?» Scoring Criteria: Clarity of process, understanding of strategic sales planning, and ability to tailor plans to specific clients.

3. **Conflict Resolution:** «Tell us about a challenging situation with a key account and how you resolved it.» Scoring Criteria: Problem-solving skills, communication effectiveness, and ability to maintain positive client relationships.

Technical Knowledge Questions

1 **Product Expertise:** «How do you stay informed about the products you are selling and the changes in the market?» Scoring Criteria: Commitment to continuous learning and strategies for staying informed.

2 **Market Analysis:** «Explain how you analyze market trends and incorporate this information into your account strategies.» Scoring Criteria: Analytical skills and the ability to translate market data into actionable strategies.

Behavioral Trait Questions

1 **Adaptability:** «Share an example when you had to adapt your approach because of changes in the market or client needs.» Scoring Criteria: Flexibility, adaptability, and responsiveness to change.

2 **Leadership:** «Describe a situation where you led a team to achieve a sales target. What was your leadership style and how did it contribute to the team's success?» Scoring Criteria: Leadership qualities, team management, and the ability to inspire and motivate others.

CONCLUSION
- Thank the candidate for their time.
- Explain the next steps in the hiring process.
- Allow the candidate to ask any questions they may have.

Remember, the key to an effective structured interview is consistency. Each candidate should be asked the same questions, and their responses should be evaluated against the same criteria. This ensures fairness and objectivity in the hiring process.

Maintaining talent density - Netflix case

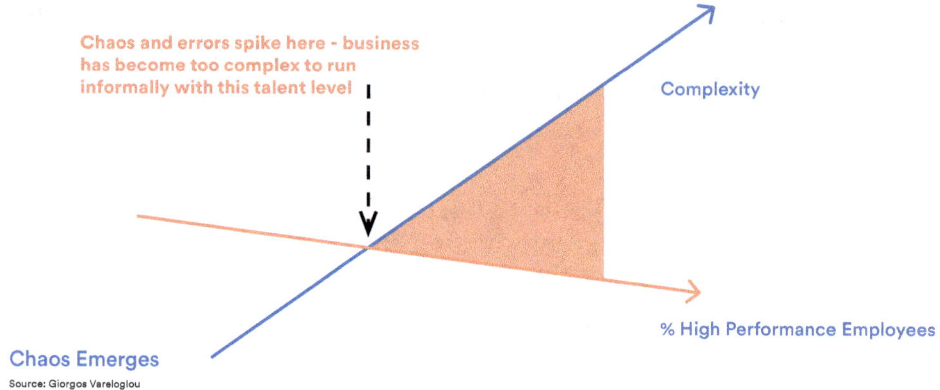

Source: Giorgos Vareloglou

In the alchemy of organizational success, the quality of the talent within your ranks is the most potent element. But like any refined substance, maintaining its density is an ongoing process that requires diligence, foresight, and strategy. This section is dedicated to the art and science of maintaining talent density within your organization. We take a look at this concept with Reed Hasting, CEO of Netflix and author of the book No Rules Rules, which popularized Talent Density. At the heart of Netflix's trailblazing corporate culture is a paradoxical blend of freedom and responsibility—a concept that has turned traditional management on its head and has been instrumental in maintaining the company's talent density.

Empowering Through Freedom

Netflix's journey teaches us that to elicit the best from your top talent, you must grant them freedom—a significant departure from micromanagement. This means allowing employees the autonomy to make decisions that they deem fit for their projects. Such freedom encourages innovation, as it empowers employees to experiment and pushes them to think outside conventional parameters.

Responsibility as a Counterbalance

However, this freedom comes with a profound sense of responsibility. Employees are expected to act in Netflix's best interests, considering the long-term implications of their decisions. It's not about spending hours at the office; it's about achieving results. Netflix, thus, does not track vacation days or approve expenses but trusts its employees to make judicious decisions. This trust, surprisingly to some, rarely leads to abuse; instead, it fosters a sense of ownership and aligns personal goals with those of the company.

Culture Over Process

Netflix maintains talent density by prioritizing culture over process. While processes can be necessary for risk mitigation, they often come at the cost of slowing down creativity and decision-making. At Netflix, the goal is to create a culture so strong that it acts as a guiding force, rendering heavy processes unnecessary.

The Keeper Test: Ensuring Talent Density

One of the most talked-about practices from Netflix is the «Keeper Test.» Managers regularly ask themselves whether they would fight to keep an employee. If the answer is no, the employee is given a generous severance package. This might seem harsh, but it ensures that the company retains only those who contribute positively to its culture and performance—thereby maintaining a high talent density.

Feedback: Candid and Regular

Candid feedback is another cornerstone of Netflix's culture. Regular, constructive feedback loops ensure that all employees, regardless of position, understand their strengths and areas for improvement. This culture of feedback is pivotal for personal growth and aligns with the company's core value of continuous improvement.

Leading by Context, Not Control

Netflix's leadership philosophy is about setting context rather than exerting control. Leaders provide the insight and understanding needed for teams to make smart decisions. The focus is on giving people the information they need to understand the larger picture, rather than prescribing the specifics of their day-to-day work.

Conclusion: A Living, Breathing Culture

Netflix's example is a testament to the fact that maintaining talent density is not a static goal but a dynamic process. It requires creating an environment where high-performing individuals are not only attracted to the company but also continually motivated to grow and contribute to its success. It's about building a culture that lives and breathes the principles of freedom, responsibility, and mutual respect—a culture where the best ideas prevail, not the biggest titles.

Crafting effective teams

Equipped with the knowledge to architect your organization, to fill it with top-tier talent, and to sustain peak talent density, you now face the critical task of orchestrating your team's collective efforts.

There are essential principles I've discerned through observation and which research corroborates. Key considerations include determining the ideal team size and understanding the composition and dynamics that fuel effective collaboration

Optimizing Team Size: Finding the Sweet Spot

The Ringelmann Effect posits that individual contribution to a group's effort starts diminishing as the team grows beyond three members. Research points towards an optimal team size of approximately 4.7 individuals. However, pragmatically speaking, I advocate adopting Jeff Bezos's «two pizza rule»: if two pizzas aren't enough to feed the entire team, it's too large. This heuristic isn't just about food; it emphasizes the importance of small, agile groups that can operate efficiently and maintain high levels of engagement.

Rigelmann Effect

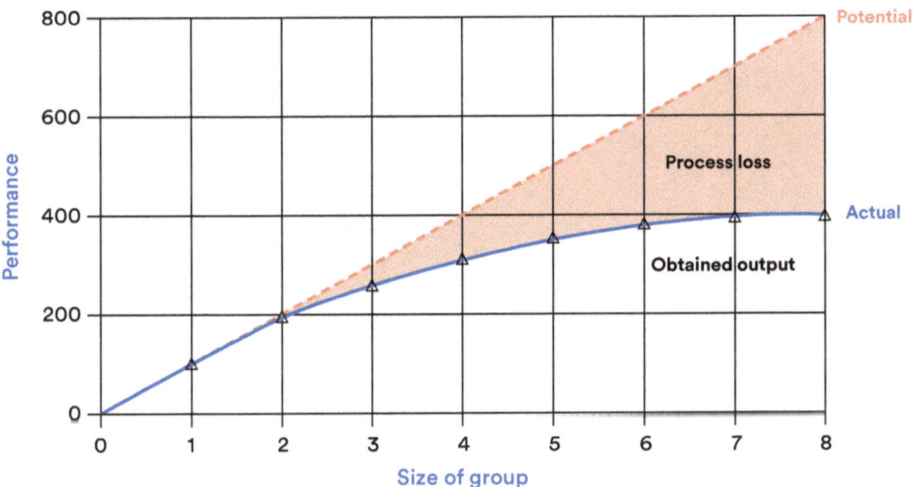

Mastering Team Dynamics

In the quest to master team dynamics, one must become a student of group psychology and recognize the evolutionary stages of a team's lifecycle. These stages, famously encapsulated by psychologist Bruce Tuckman's model, are as follows: Forming, Storming, Norming, Performing, and Adjourning. Understanding and adeptly navigating through each phase can transform a group of individuals into a unified, high-functioning team.

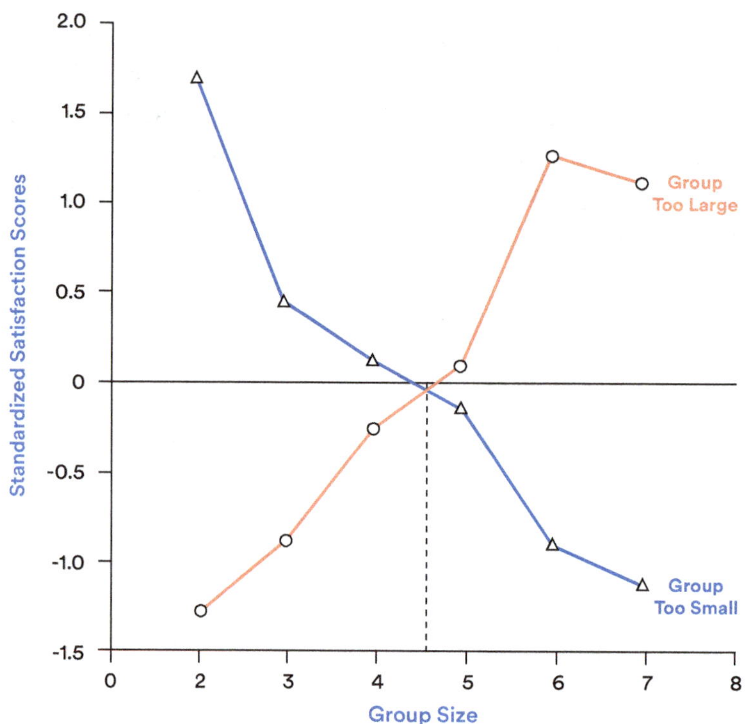

Phase of Team Development

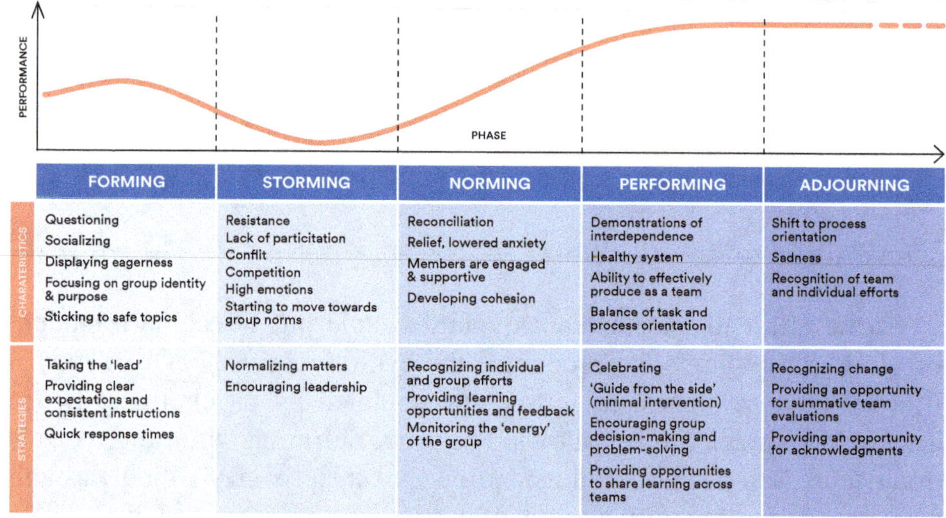

	FORMING	STORMING	NORMING	PERFORMING	ADJOURNING
CHARACTERISTICS	Questioning Socializing Displaying eagerness Focusing on group identity & purpose Sticking to safe topics	Resistance Lack of particitation Conflit Competition High emotions Starting to move towards group norms	Reconciliation Relief, lowered anxiety Members are engaged & supportive Developing cohesion	Demonstrations of interdependence Healthy system Ability to effectively produce as a team Balance of task and process orientation	Shift to process orientation Sadness Recognition of team and individual efforts
STRATEGIES	Taking the 'lead' Providing clear expectations and consistent instructions Quick response times	Normalizing matters Encouraging leadership	Recognizing individual and group efforts Providing learning opportunities and feedback Monitoring the 'energy' of the group	Celebrating 'Guide from the side' (minimal intervention) Encouraging group decision-making and problem-solving Providing opportunities to share learning across teams	Recognizing change Providing an opportunity for summative team evaluations Providing an opportunity for acknowledgments

Forming, Storming, Norming, Performing, and Adjourning - based on group development model by Bruce Tuckman
All phrases are necessary and inevitable for a team to grow, tackle problems, find solutions, plan work, and deliver results.

The 'Forming' stage is characterized by politeness, optimism, and superficiality. Team members are still independent, and as such, leadership requires a firm hand in steering the group towards its goals. The key here is to establish clear objectives, define roles, and foster an environment of openness. Leaders should be prepared to answer many questions about the team's purpose and the expectations of each member. This stage sets the groundwork for trust and camaraderie.

Conflict is not a symptom of a failing team; it is a natural occurrence in the 'Storming' stage. Here, individuals test the boundaries of group dynamics. Clashes may arise over differences in working styles or contestations of hierarchy. The leader's role becomes one of a mediator and coach, guiding the team through conflicts and ensuring that these disputes are resolved constructively. This stage is crucial for the team's growth, as it is through these trials that members learn to respect each other's perspectives and abilities.

As the team moves into the 'Norming' phase, a sense of unity begins to emerge. Members understand and appreciate the strengths of their teammates. Leadership should now focus on reinforcing this cohesion by establishing shared values and norms. Collaboration increases, and collective decision-making becomes more streamlined. The leader's involvement in decision-making can decrease as team autonomy and competence grow.

In the 'Performing' stage, the team operates like a well-oiled machine. Members are highly motivated and competent. Leadership can now delegate tasks with confidence and focus on higher-level strategic planning. The team is now able to handle complex tasks with minimal supervision. This is the pinnacle of team development, where the full potential of the collective is realized.

Finally, the 'Adjourning' stage is concerned with the disbanding of the team, once the project is complete. This phase is often overlooked but is vital for closure and reflection. Leadership should encourage team members to celebrate their successes and learn from any setbacks. Recognizing individual contributions and ensuring that members take valuable lessons forward into their next team or project is essential for ongoing development.

Each stage of the team development process is a stepping stone towards efficiency and effectiveness. As a leader, your capacity to facilitate the progression from one stage to the next, with empathy and strategic insight, will ultimately dictate the heights your team can reach. This journey of collaboration is an art form where the medium is the human element and the masterpiece is the success wrought through collective effort.

The most potent tool at your disposal to guide your team through these stages is Patrick Lencioni's «The Five Dysfunctions of a Team» framework. It's a blueprint for identifying and overcoming common hurdles that prevent teams from reaching their full potential.

Overcoming the five dysfunctions of team

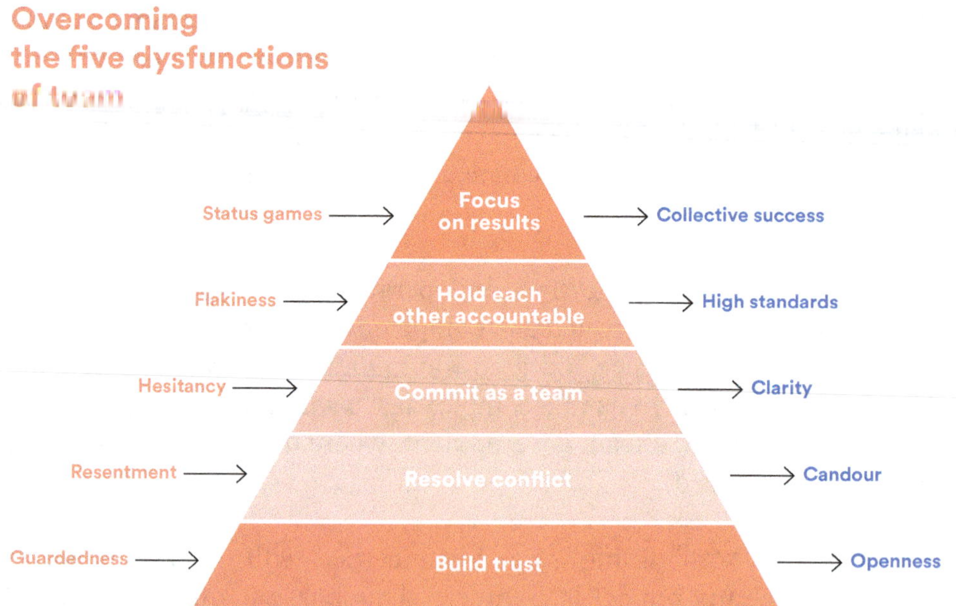

Concept by Patrick Lencioni BiteSize Learning

1 Absence of Trust

- Description: Teams that lack trust are often afraid to engage in open, constructive ideological conflicts. Instead, they resort to veiled discussions and guarded comments.
- How to Address: Promote healthy debates as a source of productive team interactions. Establish clear norms that differentiate respectful disagreement from personal attacks, ensuring that conflicts are focused on ideas and decisions, not individuals.

2 Fear of Conflict

- Description: Teams that lack trust are often afraid to engage in open, constructive ideological conflicts. Instead, they resort to veiled discussions and guarded comments.
- How to Address: Promote healthy debates as a source of productive team interactions. Establish clear norms that differentiate respectful disagreement from personal attacks, ensuring that conflicts are focused on ideas and decisions, not individuals.

3 Lack of Commitment

- Description: A team that does not engage in open conflict will often experience a lack of commitment to decisions, as not all opinions and viewpoints have been considered. This leads to ambiguity among the team about direction and priorities.
- How to Address: Foster clarity and closure around decisions, even in the face of incomplete information. Encourage team members to voice their opinions during decision-making processes, ensuring that all views are considered and helping to secure buy-in even from those who may initially disagree.

4 Avoidance of Accountability

- Description: Without a clear commitment to a plan of action, team members often hesitate to call out peers on actions and behaviors that seem counterproductive to the team's good
- How to Address: Foster clarity and closure around decisions, even in the face of incomplete information. Encourage team members to voice their opinions during decision-making pro-

cesses, ensuring that all views are considered and helping to secure buy-in even from those who may initially disagree.

⑤ Inattention to Results

- Description: The ultimate dysfunction of a team occurs when members place their individual needs (such as ego, career development, or recognition) or even the needs of their divisions above the collective goals of the team.
- How to Address: Align team objectives with the overall success of the organization. Celebrate collective successes and make the team's results the ultimate measure of effectiveness. Ensure that personal goals and team goals are aligned so that achieving team results also means meeting personal objectives.

By systematically addressing each of these dysfunctions, teams can move towards a more cohesive, effective, and high-performing state. I carried out the assessment after renewing the majority of my executive team. This enabled me to address problems much more quickly, so that I could rely on them when my first child arrived

Igniting Momentum: Urgency and Cadence

To set the wheels of high performance in motion, instill a sense of urgency and establish a fitting cadence. The right tempo for your team's activities can foster a shared understanding that time is of the essence, galvanizing the group into action. This doesn't mean rushing decisions or processes, but rather creating an environment where complacency has no quarter, and excellence is pursued with vigor. Statistics show that a sense of urgency can increase team performance by up to 51%, according to a study by the Corporate Executive Board. Urgency is the spark that ignites action, while cadence is the rhythm that maintains the flame, ensuring that it burns steadily and brightly.

Urgency is a powerful motivator. A Harvard Business Review article highlighted that teams with a high sense of urgency were more proactive, innovative, and responsive to change. To create this, a leader must communicate the vision and importance of the mission with clarity. For example, when Steve Jobs returned to Apple in 1997, he instilled a sense of urgency by focusing on a few key products and pushing for excellence in design and function. This urgency led to the development of groundbreaking products like the iPod, which revolutionized the music industry.

Cadence, on the other hand, provides the consistent beat that keeps the team's progress on track. A study by the Project Management Institute found that teams with a strong, regular cadence were 33% more likely to meet their goals. In practice, this means establishing regular check-ins, deadlines, and milestones. Remember Jeff Bezos, with his «two-pizza teams»? Ill ensured that the small size of the team facilitated quick meetings and decisions, enabling Amazon to innovate quickly. So pair this cadence with the right team sizing.

At Neobrain, as we grew and passed the 100-employee mark, we saw a decline in meaningful engagement. We introduced WeLoveMondays, a 30-minute get-together for the whole company at 5pm on Mondays. This sequence is meticulously prepared in advance, during which we make product announcements, celebrate signings, focus on the main reasons for lost deals to improve, and so on. This sequence remains important to align the whole company on the same dynamic.

A prime example of the successful implementation of urgency and cadence can be observed in the software industry. Agile methodologies, like Scrum, use sprints—short, consistent work cycles—to maintain a steady pace of development. This method was employed by Spotify to great effect, allowing it to adapt quickly and release new features regularly, staying ahead of competitors.

Another illustration comes from the world of emergency services. Firefighters operate with a sense of urgency out of necessity, and their work is underpinned by a strict cadence of training and maintenance schedules. This ensures that when the alarm sounds, the team is ready to act without hesitation.

The challenge for leaders is to balance urgency and cadence. Too much urgency can lead to burnout, while an overly relaxed cadence can lead to stagnation. The balance was masterfully achieved by the 2008 Beijing Olympic Games organizers, who managed thousands of volunteers and hundreds of events with precision. This was possible through meticulous planning and the cultivation of a sense of urgency around the global importance of the Games.

In conclusion, urgency compels a team to take off, while cadence ensures they soar at the right altitude. It's the leader's role to strike this delicate balance, creating a rhythm that harmonizes the talents of the team, driving them toward excellence.

Chapter 10

Using AI to accelerate your business growth - Go-to-market strategies

The AI revolution in sales and marketing: to your weapons

As a successful entrepreneur, mastering growth management is paramount, yet it's not just about growing at any cost. The cornerstone of this strategy is the «Sales & Marketing efficiency ratio,» a pivotal metric that businesses must deftly navigate to outperform industry norms.

Here, the early adoption of technologies like Machine Learning and GenAI isn't just a competitive advantage—it's a critical imperative. These cutting-edge tools promise to redefine the landscape of competitiveness, provided businesses focus on high-priority use cases and the necessary organizational changes to integrate them effectively.

The realm of sales and marketing stands out as a fertile ground for AI-driven creativity. As we step into 2024, the directory «There's an AI for That» lists an impressive 6,568 AI solutions impacting this area. But what's the real score on the adoption of these groundbreaking tools? While marketing and sales leaders are beginning to harness AI for specific applications, there's a widely held belief that the technology remains underutilized. A McKinsey study reveals that 55% of sales teams seldom use generative AI, whereas 90% of sales directors believe their teams should always or often utilize GenAI or machine learning. This gap highlights an incredible playground for entrepreneurs to turn this technology into a decisive competitive edge.

Commercial leaders are already leveraging gen AI use cases - but most feel the technology is underutilized

Extent to which commercial leaders feel their organizations are using machine learning/gen AI, [1] % of responses

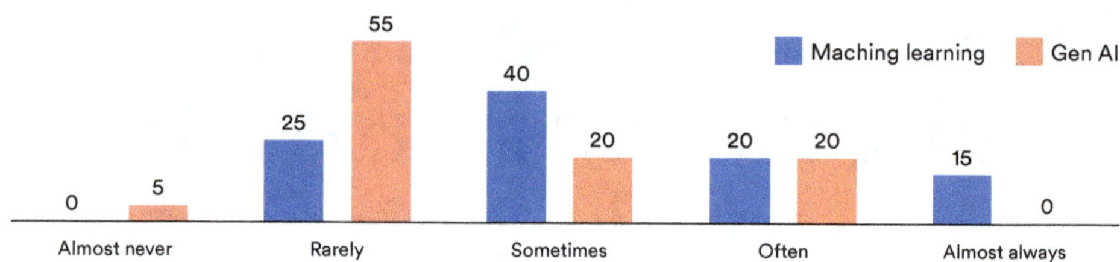

Extent to which commercial leaders think their organizations schould be using machine learning/gen AI, [2] % of responses

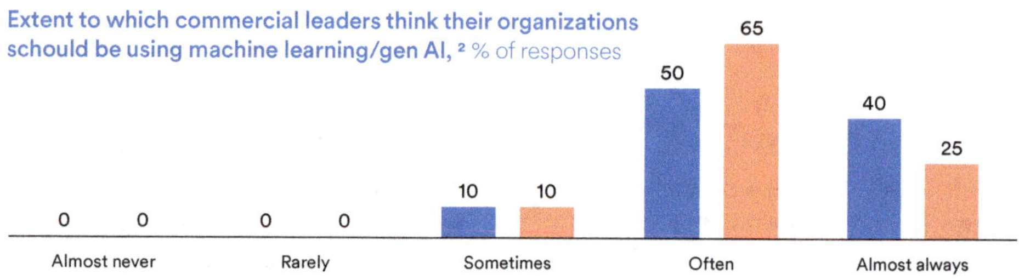

1Senior executives in significant global B2B and B2C sales and marketing organizations across a wide range of industries and company maturity levels were asked: To what extent is your organization using ML / gen AI solution? - 2Q: How much do you think your organization should be using ML / gen AI solution? - Source: McKinsey analysis

According to McKinsey, AI is set to revolutionize marketing and sales across all sectors. The firm predicts that generative AI could boost marketing productivity by 5% to 15% across various applications, including large-scale personalized content creation, enhanced customer engagement, deeper customer and data insights, and more efficient lead identification and development.

So, where to begin? The top three use cases that are poised to make the most significant impact are:

1 Real-time lead identification, based on consumer trends,

2 Marketing optimization through A/B testing and SEO strategies,

3 Personalized outreach with chatbots and virtual assistants.

Commercial leaders are already leveraging gen AI use cases - but most feel the technology is underutilized

Estimated impact of use cases, [1] % of respondents answering "significant" or "very significant"

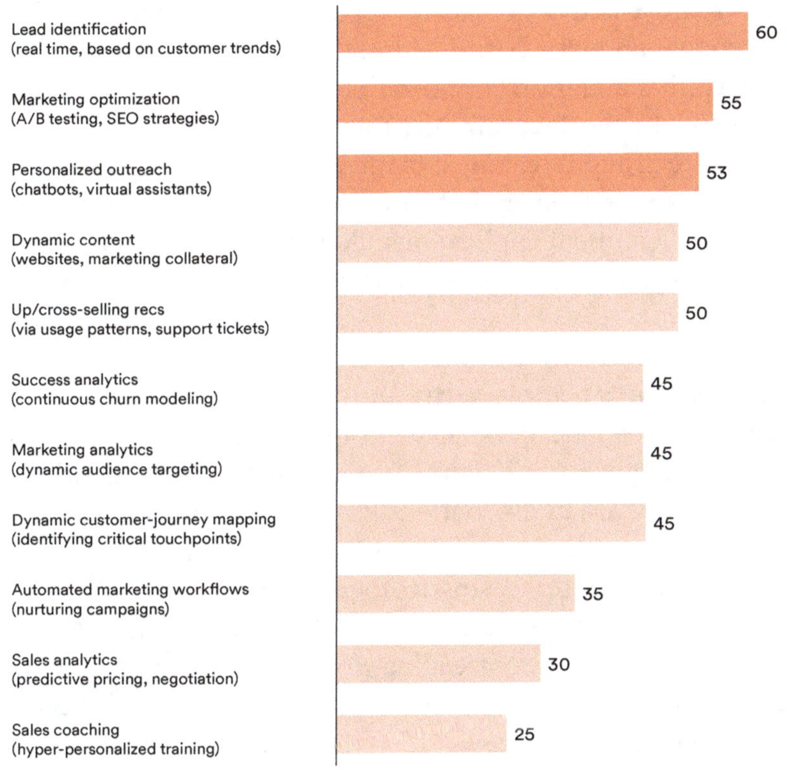

1Senior executives in significant global B2B and B2C sales and marketing organizations across a wide range of industries and company maturity levels were asked: Please share your estimated ROI / impact these tools would have if implemented is your organization. - Source: McKinsey analysis

In the continuation of this chapter, I won't delve into new concepts or theoretical models but will instead highlight concrete use cases and technologies that can accelerate your business. I'll share a personal experiment: creating a website entirely powered by AI that detects trending topics, writes, and publishes articles to build a community. This example perfectly illustrates how artificial intelligence can serve as a powerful lever to energize your business in the competitive sales and marketing arena.

AI Unleashed: Transformative Sales Strategies That Will Leave You Astonished

McKinsey's latest findings deliver a startling revelation: one out of every five sales representatives could be replaced by the productivity enhancements brought about by Artificial Intelligence (AI). This statistic isn't just a forecast; it's a clarion call to action, signaling a pivotal shift in the sales domain. In the face of such transformative potential, I'm poised to unveil three groundbreaking examples of how Generative AI is not just enhancing sales efficiency but turbocharging business traction. These are not mere theoretical applications; they are practical, powerful tools that are redefining what's possible in sales strategy and execution.

1 Personalization at Scale with Quick.ai

Imagine a world where the first point of contact for your clients isn't just personalized; it's uniquely tailored to each individual. Quick.ai, akin to ChatGPT but customized with your own data model, is making this a reality. It streamlines initial client qualification, allowing sales teams to focus their energies where it matters most. An illustrative example is Preface Factory's AI assistant, trained on best proofreading practices to support authors through the tedious task of revision, showcasing AI's ability to personalize complex processes.

2 Mojo: Elevating Sales Performance through Knowledge Sharing

The journey from onboarding a new sales representative to full productivity is fraught with inefficiencies. Mojo revolutionizes this process by automating the transcription of sales calls and summarizing notes through AI. This not only facilitates knowledge sharing but also enables sales leaders to pinpoint deals at risk by analyzing client call dynamics. The transformation here is profound, reducing ramp-up times and enhancing sales performance through insights that were previously inaccessible.

③ Bland.ai: The Frontier of Automated, Personalized Outreach

Perhaps the most astonishing application of AI in sales is embodied by Bland.ai. This platform can execute 10,000 calls simultaneously, all powered by AI, creating a user experience so seamless that participants believe they're conversing with a human. This technology was put to the test in the HR tech domain with Neobrain, demonstrating its capability to handle objections more adeptly than a seasoned sales rep. By leveraging a portion of the company's knowledge base, Bland.ai managed objections with unparalleled finesse, showcasing the futuristic potential of AI in sales engagement.

These examples are not mere predictions; they are realities unfolding in the present, marking a paradigm shift in how sales strategies are conceived and executed. The statistics supporting these innovations speak volumes, with AI-driven personalization leading to an average increase in customer engagement rates by up to 40%, according to Salesforce. Furthermore, companies that have integrated AI into their sales processes report a 50% reduction in lead qualification times, as found in a study by IBM.

As we stand on the brink of this new era, the message is clear: AI is not just transforming sales strategies—it's catapulting them into a realm of efficiency, personalization, and performance previously unimaginable. The companies that harness these technologies today will not only gain a competitive edge but will redefine the benchmarks of success in the sales domain.

Marketing Reimagined: Groundbreaking AI Applications That Will Amaze You

In the dynamic world of digital marketing, the integration of AI technologies has not just been a game-changer; it's redefined the playing field. Let's delve into two revolutionary examples that showcase how AI can dramatically enhance marketing efforts, creating high-impact results with minimal effort and investment.

① Revolutionizing Video Content with Heygen

Imagine the ability to produce personalized, engaging video content at scale, without the need for a sophisticated studio setup or extensive production time. Tools like Heygen and Synthesia have made this a reality. By combining the prowess of ChatGPT for scripting and these platforms for video creation, marketers can now churn out high-quality videos in minutes. This democratization of video production allows businesses of any size to leverage video marketing, one of the most effective content formats today, with unprecedented ease and efficiency. The implications are vast: from skyrocketing engagement rates to significantly lowering the cost and barriers to entry in video marketing.

② The Automated Community Builder

The power of community in marketing cannot be overstated. A vibrant community not only amplifies your marketing efforts but also provides a fertile ground for feedback and loyalty. However, building such a community traditionally requires considerable time and resources—until now. My experiment in creating a self-growing community focused on AI demonstrates the potential of AI-driven tools in achieving this with virtually no daily time investment.

Here's how I did it:
- Choosing the niche: AI, in preparation for launching my second book post «Will AI Replace Me.».
- Setting up a platform: I established a WordPress site.
- Content generation: Utilized auto-blogger plugins to automatically draft and publish articles on trending AI topics
- Market intelligence: Integrated SemRush for automatic market and keyword trend monitoring, further connecting it to the

auto-blogger via an iPaaS for seamless content relevance and optimization.
- SEO optimization: Applied SEO diagnostic tools to enhance site visibility.

The result? ai-inspiration.com now autonomously publishes 2-3 in-depth articles daily, securing key SEO positions and drawing 700-1000 unique visitors monthly. This groundwork ensures an engaged community ready for my book launch, predicting a traffic surge to 4000 unique visitors monthly. With a conservative conversion rate of 1%, this equates to an additional €13,000 in book sales annually—all from a single day's setup and zero maintenance.

These examples underscore a critical message: the integration of AI in marketing is not just about efficiency; it's about opening new avenues for engagement, community building, and ultimately, revenue generation. With concrete statistics and proven methodologies, the message is clear: the future of marketing lies in the smart, strategic application of AI technologies.

3

Build your business in the AI arena

As we transition from Part II, equipped with the knowledge and strategies to supercharge your business through AI shortcuts, we approach an even more thrilling juncture in our journey. Part III is designed to deep dive into the very heart of the AI market, unraveling the dynamics, forecasting the future, and unveiling the plethora of opportunities that lie in creating a business within the AI arena.

The AI landscape is not just evolving; it's exploding in terms of both innovation and market size. To put this into perspective, consider the staggering growth trajectory of the U.S. artificial intelligence market. From a substantial base of USD 103.7 billion in 2022, it's projected to balloon to an astounding USD 594 billion by 2032, charting a Compound Annual Growth Rate (CAGR) of 19.1% from 2023 to 2032. This meteoric rise underscores not just the potential but the necessity for entrepreneurs and business leaders to understand and engage with AI at a foundational level.

In Part III, we're not merely observing from the sidelines; we're plunging into the core of AI's market dynamics. We'll explore the underlying forces propelling this growth, dissect the sectors ripe for disruption, and spotlight the emerging technologies that promise to redefine industries. This section is your blueprint to navigating the vibrant AI landscape, identifying untapped opportunities, and positioning yourself at the forefront of the AI revolution.

Prepare to embark on a journey to the future, where AI is not a distant dream but an accessible, transformative reality. Welcome to Part III: Building Your Business in the AI Arena.

Chapter 11
Decoding the AI Market

The AI revolution in sales and marketing: to your weapons

The artificial intelligence (AI) landscape is a vast and complex field, characterized by rapid technological advancements and a wide array of applications across various industries. Understanding the market structure is crucial for businesses, investors, and innovators aiming to navigate this space effectively. This chapter delves into the eight different segments of the AI market, highlighting their roles, interactions, and the dynamics that drive the development and adoption of AI technologies.

1 **Technology Providers: The Foundation of AI**

Technology providers form the backbone of the AI market, encompassing a broad spectrum of entities that develop the underlying technologies enabling AI applications. This segment is divided into three main categories.

  a. AI Software Developers: These are the companies and organizations that create the algorithms, machine learning models, and software frameworks that power AI applications. Giants like Google, Microsoft, IBM, and OpenAI are at the forefront, offering advanced AI capabilities to the market.

  b. Hardware Manufacturers: Specialized AI hardware is critical for the efficient processing of complex algorithms. This category includes producers of GPUs, TPUs, and AI-specific chips, with NVIDIA, Intel, and AMD leading the pack. Their products are essential for running AI applications efficiently.

c. AI Services Providers: Offering AI-as-a-Service, these organizations provide cloud-based AI platforms, APIs, and tools that enable developers and businesses to leverage AI capabilities without significant upfront investment in hardware or development. Amazon Web Services, Microsoft Azure, and Google Cloud are prominent players, facilitating access to powerful AI resources.

② Applications and Use Cases: AI in Action

AI finds application across a multitude of industries, transforming operations, enhancing efficiency, and creating new user experiences. This segment is vast, but notable applications include :

a. Industry-Specific Solutions: From healthcare and finance to automotive and manufacturing, AI technologies are tailored to meet the unique challenges and opportunities within each sector.

b. Consumer Applications: AI enriches consumer products and services, evident in virtual assistants, recommendation systems, and autonomous vehicles, making technology more intuitive and personalized.

c. Specialized Domains: Areas like healthcare, finance, e-commerce, and manufacturing have witnessed significant transformations through AI, with innovations in medical imaging, fraud detection, personalized shopping experiences, and automation of production processes.

③ AI Services and Consulting: Bridging Gaps

As AI technologies become more sophisticated, the need for expert guidance and tailored solutions has grown. AI consulting firms and educational institutions play a pivotal role in this context by offering advisory, implementation services, and training. This segment ensures that businesses can effectively integrate AI into their operations, overcoming technical and strategic challenges.

4 Regulatory and Ethical Agencies: Guiding Responsible AI

The rapid adoption of AI technologies brings forth critical ethical and regulatory considerations. Government agencies, along with ethical AI advocacy groups, work to establish frameworks and guidelines that ensure the responsible development and deployment of AI. This segment addresses issues related to data privacy, bias, and safety, ensuring AI advances in a manner that is ethical and compliant with societal norms.

5 Research and Development: Pushing Boundaries

The quest for innovation in AI is relentless, with academic institutions and corporate research labs leading the charge. This segment is essential for the continued advancement of AI, exploring new theories, models, and applications. Collaborations at this level often set the stage for breakthrough technologies that redefine what's possible with AI.

6 Investors and Funding: Fueling Growth

The AI market's expansion is significantly driven by investment from venture capitalists, corporate entities, and other financial backers. This segment provides the capital necessary for research, development, and scaling of AI technologies, enabling startups and established companies alike to push the boundaries of innovation.

7 AI Marketplaces and Platforms: Facilitating Access

To democratize access to AI technologies, marketplaces and development platforms serve as crucial intermediaries. These platforms connect AI developers and solution providers with businesses and consumers seeking AI-powered enhancements, streamlining the deployment and integration of AI applications.

8 The AI Talent Pool: The Human Element

At the heart of the AI market are the individuals who design, develop, and deploy AI technologies. Data scientists, machine learning engineers, AI researchers, and developers constitute this vital segment, driving innovation and ensuring the practical application of AI across various domains.

Each segment presents unique growth prospects and entry barriers, shaping the strategic decisions for new and existing ventures.

Market Structure & Opportunities in the AI Arena

CATEGORY	PREDICTED TREND	ENTRY BARRIER
Technology Providers	High Growth	High (Technical Expertise & Capital)
Applications and Use Cases	High Growth	Moderate to High (Industry Knowledge & Partnerships)
AI Services and Consulting	Moderate Growth	Moderate (Expertise in AI and Market Knowledge)
Regulatory and Ethical Considerations	Increasing Importance	High (Understanding of Legal & Ethical Standards)
Research and Development	High Growth	High (Innovative Research & Development)
Investors and Funding	Steady Growth	Moderate to High (Access to Capital & Investment Acumen)
AI Marketplaces and Platforms	High Growth	Moderate (Platform Development & Network)
The AI Talent Pool	Critical Demand	Low to Moderate (Talent Development & Retention)

Key Trends and Insights

Technology Providers and Applications & Use Cases stand out with their rapid advancement, driven by the escalating demand for cutting-edge AI solutions, albeit with significant technical and financial entry barriers. Research and Development, along with AI Marketplaces and Platforms, promise substantial growth, fueled by innovation and the democratization of AI technologies. The AI Talent Pool is expanding, offering opportunities with relatively lower entry barriers in education and talent development. Regulatory and Ethical Considerations are increasingly pivotal, presenting challenges in navigating complex standards but are essential for sustainable AI integration. Meanwhile, Investors and Funding remain crucial for fueling AI ventures, highlighting the importance of strategic investments. Collectively, these insights underscore the need for strategic positioning and understanding of market dynamics to capitalize on the high-growth opportunities within the AI industry, despite the varied challenges of entry barriers.

Understanding the AI market structure is akin to navigating a complex ecosystem, where each segment plays a distinct role yet is interconnected with the rest. The synergy between technology providers, applications, services, regulatory bodies, and the talent pool fuels the growth and evolution of AI, making it one of the most dynamic and transformative areas of the modern economy. On the other hand, AI is not neutral and its acceptability is not equivalent from one country and culture to another.

The Surprising Lead of Emerging Markets in AI Acceptance

A fascinating trend has emerged, challenging conventional wisdom about technology adoption across the globe. While one might expect the most advanced economies to lead in embracing AI, recent studies suggest that it's the emerging markets that are at the forefront of AI acceptance. This chapter delves into the reasons behind this phenomenon, its implications, and what it tells us about the future of AI globally.

Traditionally, technological innovations have found fertile ground in developed nations, with their robust infrastructure, high-income levels, and tech-savvy populations. However, AI's journey tells a different story. Countries classified as emerging markets exhibit a higher trust in AI solutions, integrating them into their daily lives and industries more readily than seen in more developed economies. This shift is not just about technology itself but reflects deeper socio-economic dynamics, aspirations, and the unique challenges these countries face.

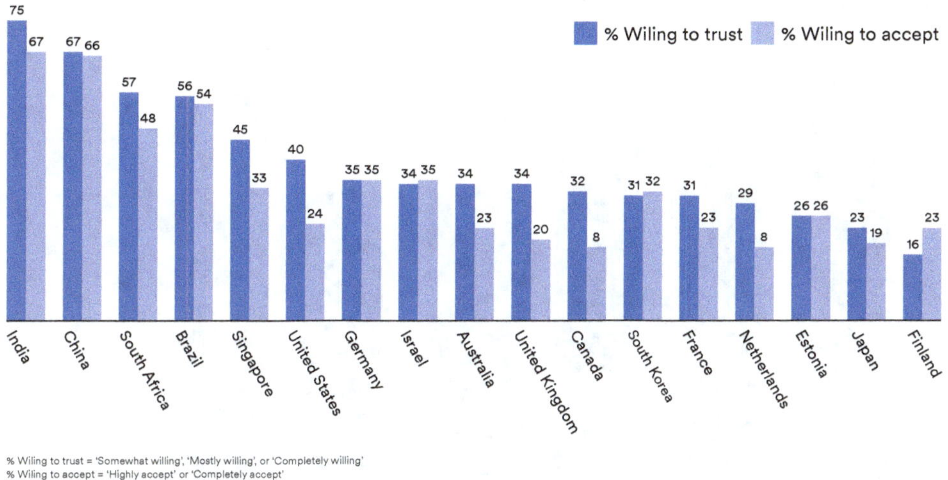

Several factors contribute to this trend. Firstly, the necessity-driven innovation in these regions often leads to a leapfrog effect. With fewer legacy systems in place, emerging markets adopt the latest technologies directly, bypassing intermediary steps that might slow down developed countries. Secondly, the pressing needs for scalable solutions in healthcare, education, and financial services make AI not just attractive but essential. AI applications offer unprecedented opportunities to address long-standing issues of access and quality in these critical sectors.

Moreover, the demographic dividend in many emerging economies, characterized by a young, adaptable, and increasingly digital-native population, creates a conducive environment for AI technologies to take root and flourish. The enthusiasm and openness to digital transformation among these younger demographics further accelerate AI's integration into societal norms.

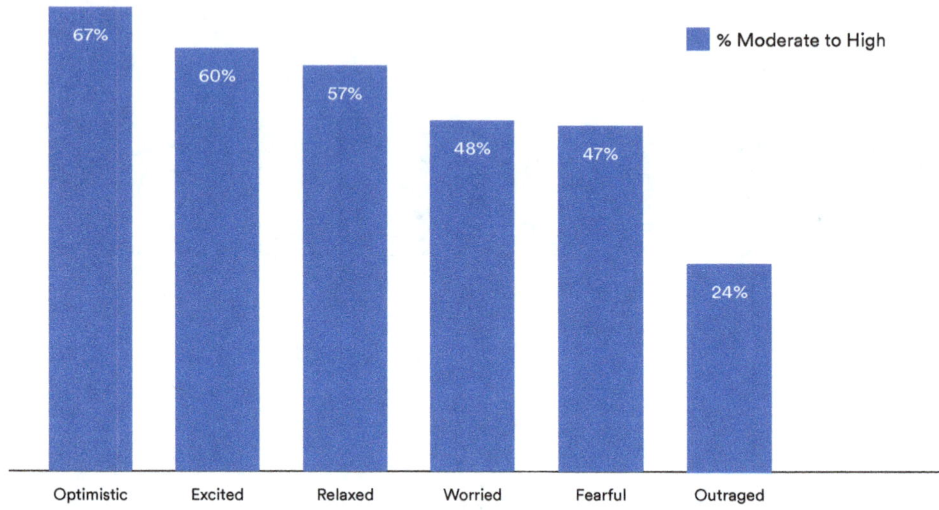

The enthusiastic adoption of AI in emerging markets has profound implications for the global economy and the AI development landscape. It challenges the traditional centers of technology innovation to rethink their strategies and offers emerging markets the chance to lead in specific AI niches. Furthermore, it democratizes AI development, bringing diverse perspectives and needs into the design and deployment of AI solutions, which is crucial for creating inclusive and universally beneficial AI technologies.

Additionally, this trend underscores the importance of global cooperation in AI ethics and governance. As AI becomes more deeply integrated into societies worldwide, ensuring these technologies are developed and used in ways that respect human rights and promote inclusivity becomes increasingly critical. Emerging markets, with their firsthand experience of AI's potential and pitfalls, will be vital voices in these global discussions.

Chapter 12
AI application users and growth

The Data Behind the AI Surge

Skeptics might still question the staying power of generative AI, but the numbers speak for themselves. ChatGPT's meteoric rise is a testament to its broad appeal and utility:

- Within its first week, ChatGPT attracted over one million users.
- By two months, it boasted 100 million active users.
- Now, with its integration into free Microsoft tools, browser sidebars, and even Windows 11 OS, ChatGPT's reach extends to a user base exceeding a billion.

This isn't just a passing trend; it's a pivotal moment in the evolution of AI, akin to how Netscape marked the internet's interface moment. ChatGPT serves as the gateway for millions into the vast potential of AI, marking a seismic shift in how technology is accessed and utilized.

You're probably wondering whether this is just a passing fad, or whether AI will come down from its hype cycle. To give you a better idea of the wave that's about to break, here are a few points of comparison with the adoption of the tools you use every day:

of days to M and 100M users by technology

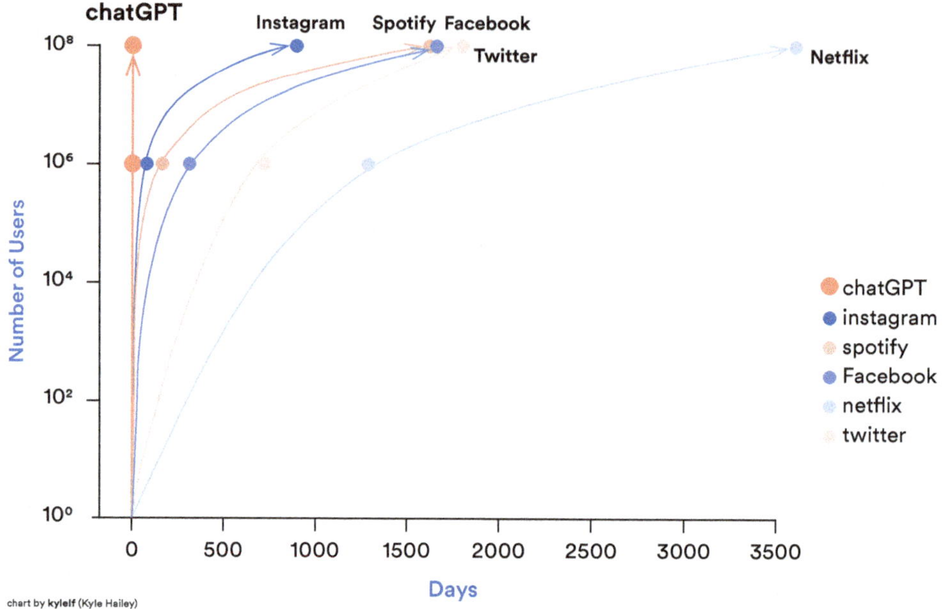

Chat-GPT sprints to 100 million users

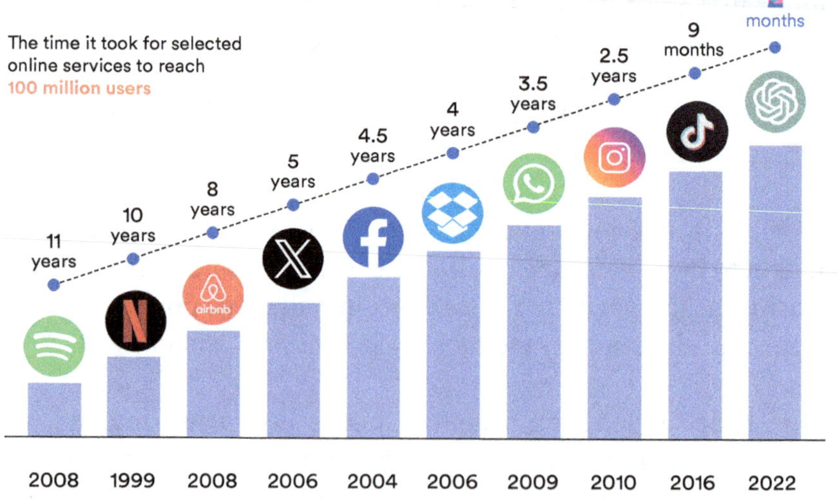

Who are the GenAI users - the case of ChatGPT

The demographic landscape of ChatGPT users offers a fascinating glimpse into the generational embrace of artificial intelligence. A study, drawing from Statista's comprehensive analytics, sheds light on the gender distribution, age demographics, and geographical dispersion of ChatGPT's user base, painting a detailed picture of those at the forefront of interacting with this groundbreaking technology.

The gender split among ChatGPT users is relatively balanced, with males representing 55.06% of the user base, while females account for 44.94%. This near parity underscores the wide-reaching appeal and accessibility of ChatGPT across gender lines, highlighting its role as a versatile tool for a diverse range of applications.

A significant majority of ChatGPT users fall within the younger age brackets, indicative of the millennial and Gen Z generations' propensity for early adoption of new technologies. Specifically, 64.53% of users are between the ages of 18 and 34, with the distribution as follows:

18-24 years old: 30.09%

25-34 years old: 34.44%

35-44 years old: 17.65%

45-54 years old: 9.37%

55-64 years old: 5.34%

65+ years old: 3.11%

Gender Distribution

Age Distribution

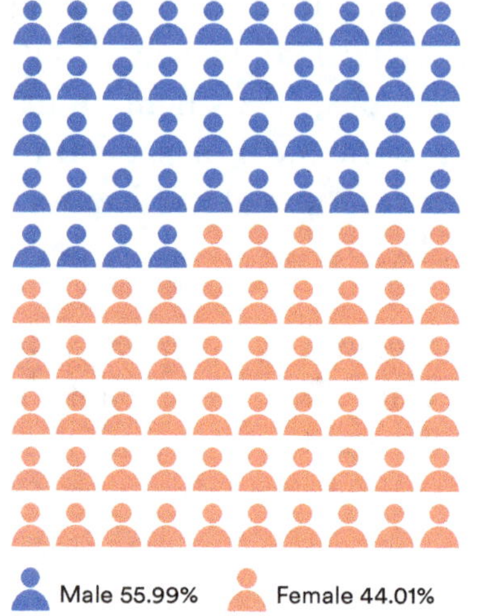

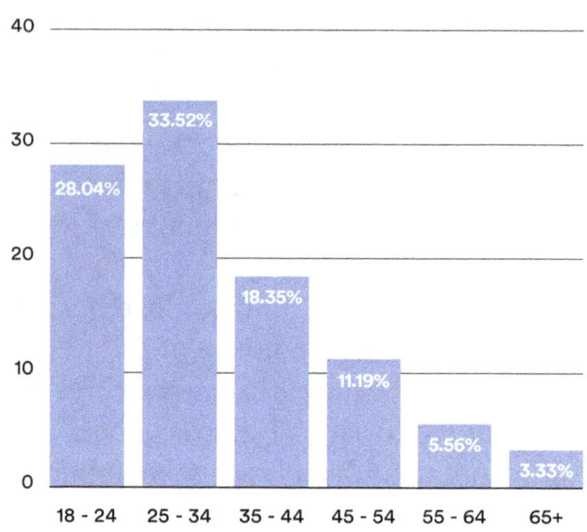

This skew towards younger users highlights the generational shift in technology use and reliance on AI for both personal and professional needs.

ChatGPT Use in Fall Quarter 2022 Finals

Brainstorming, Outlining, and forming ideas

59.2%

Answered multiple-choice questions with the help of ChatGPT

29.1%

Submitted written material from ChatGPT with edits

7.3%

Submitted written material from ChatGPT without edits

5.5%

ChatGPT's user base spans across the globe, with the United States leading at 14.4%, followed by India at 6.9%, and Columbia at 3.56%. The Philippines and Japan also feature prominently, with 3.49% and 2.96% of users, respectively. The remainder of the user base, constituting 68.69%, is distributed across various other countries, illustrating the global reach and appeal of ChatGPT.

Active ChatGPT Users in Top Coutries

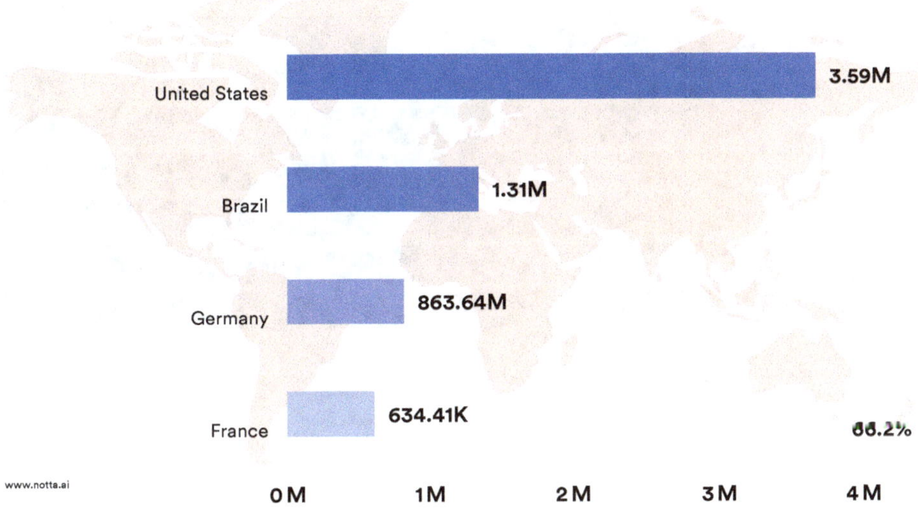

The demographic data on ChatGPT users not only provides insight into who is utilizing this technology but also signals broader trends in the adoption and application of artificial intelligence. The predominance of younger users suggests a growing comfort and reliance on AI for a myriad of tasks, from academic assistance to professional development and entertainment. Moreover, the geographical diversity of ChatGPT's user base highlights the universal appeal and potential of AI to transcend cultural and linguistic barriers, offering personalized and accessible solutions to a global audience.

In summary, the case of ChatGPT's users reflects a broader narrative of generational AI adoption, with significant implications for the future of technology engagement across different spheres of life. As AI continues to evolve, understanding these demographic trends will be crucial for Next-Gen AI Founders in harnessing the potential of GenAI to meet diverse global needs.

Nearly half of Americans have heard a lot or a little about ChatGPT

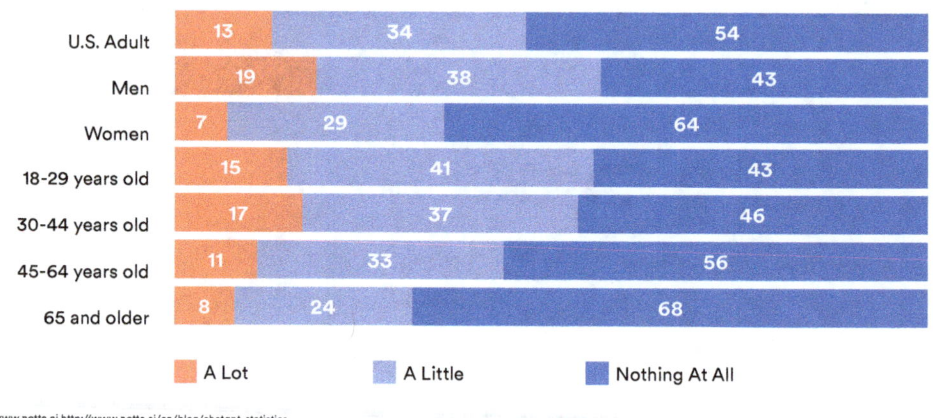

www.notta.ai http://www.notta.ai/en/blog/chatgpt-statistics

AI application users and growth

The most promising industries

As artificial intelligence continues to evolve, its impact across various sectors is becoming increasingly profound, offering lucrative opportunities for entrepreneurs and innovators. A recent McKinsey study sheds light on the industries where AI, particularly generative AI, holds the most promise. Among these, three stand out due to their potential for transformation and value creation: consumer packaged goods (CPG), banking, and pharmaceuticals and medical products. Each of these sectors presents unique challenges and opportunities, with AI poised to revolutionize operations, enhance customer experiences, and drive unprecedented levels of innovation.

Generative AI use cases will have different impacts on business functions across industries.

Generative AI productivity impact by business functions[1]

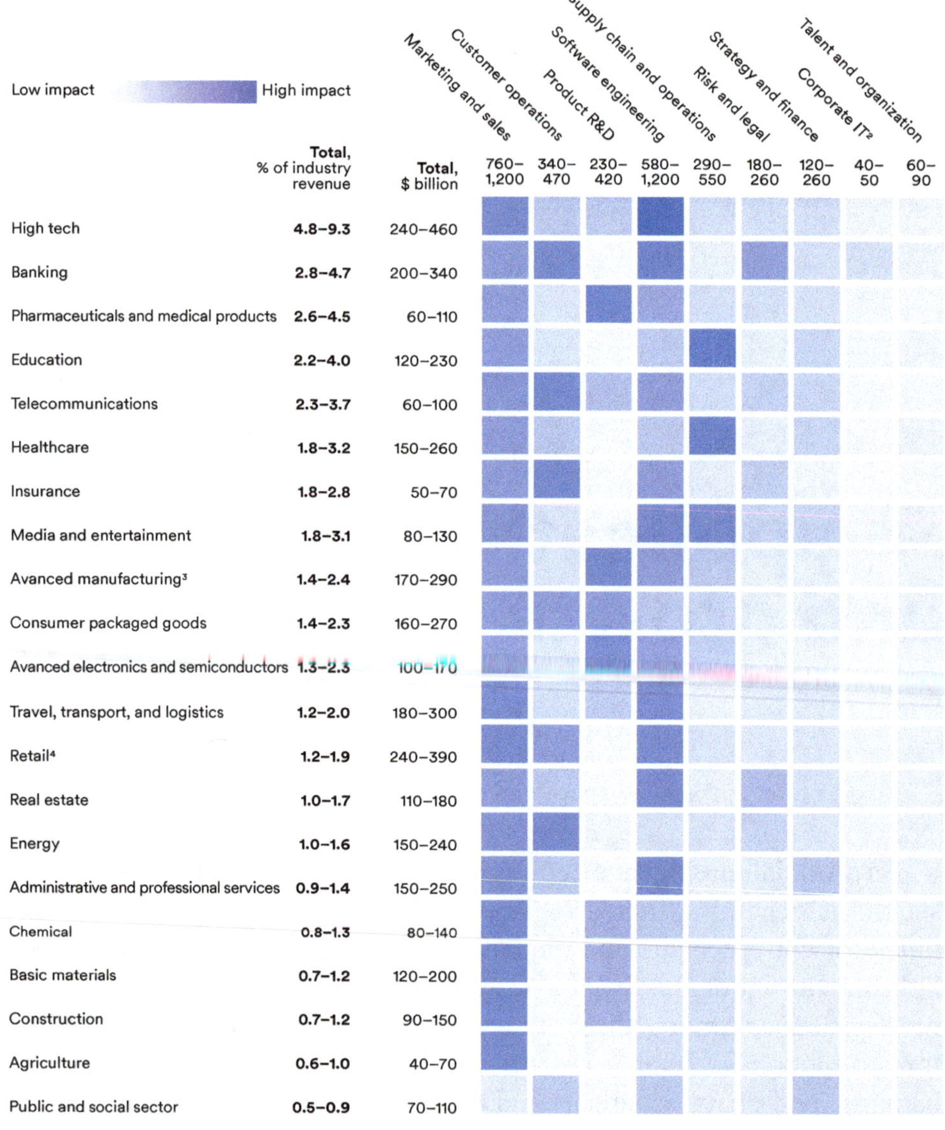

Industry	Total, % of industry revenue	Total, $ billion	Marketing and sales 760–1,200	Customer operations 340–470	Product R&D 230–420	Software engineering 580–1,200	Supply chain and operations 290–550	Risk and legal 180–260	Strategy and finance 120–260	Corporate IT[2] 40–50	Talent and organization 60–90
High tech	4.8–9.3	240–460									
Banking	2.8–4.7	200–340									
Pharmaceuticals and medical products	2.6–4.5	60–110									
Education	2.2–4.0	120–230									
Telecommunications	2.3–3.7	60–100									
Healthcare	1.8–3.2	150–260									
Insurance	1.8–2.8	50–70									
Media and entertainment	1.8–3.1	80–130									
Avanced manufacturing[3]	1.4–2.4	170–290									
Consumer packaged goods	1.4–2.3	160–270									
Avanced electronics and semiconductors	1.3–2.3	100–170									
Travel, transport, and logistics	1.2–2.0	180–300									
Retail[4]	1.2–1.9	240–390									
Real estate	1.0–1.7	110–180									
Energy	1.0–1.6	150–240									
Administrative and professional services	0.9–1.4	150–250									
Chemical	0.8–1.3	80–140									
Basic materials	0.7–1.2	120–200									
Construction	0.7–1.2	90–150									
Agriculture	0.6–1.0	40–70									
Public and social sector	0.5–0.9	70–110									
		2,600–4,400									

Note: Figures may not sum to 100%, because of rounding. 1 Excludes implementation costs (eg, training, licenses). 2 Excluding software engineering. 3 Includes aerospace, defense, and auto manufacturing. 4 Including auto retail. Source: Comparative Industry Service (CIS), IHS Markit; Oxford Economics; McKinsey Corporate and Bisiness Functions database; McKinsey Manufacturing and Supply Chain 360; McKinsey Sales Navigator; Ignite, a McKinsey database; McKinsey analysis

① Consumer goods

With an estimated value increase of 1.2 to 2.0 percent of annual revenues, translating to an additional $400 billion to $660 billion, the stakes are high and the rewards, significant. This section explores how generative AI is reshaping the CPG industry, from revolutionizing customer interactions to accelerating value creation and innovation.

The CPG industry, inherently customer-centric, is witnessing a paradigm shift in consumer engagement, thanks to generative AI. Personalization, the cornerstone of modern retail, is reaching new heights with AI's ability to tailor shopping experiences, product recommendations, and marketing strategies to individual consumer preferences. For instance, Stitch Fix's use of DALL·E to create visual product suggestions showcases the innovative ways in which generative AI can enhance customer service and satisfaction. The ability of AI to interact with consumers in a human-like manner, providing personalized advice and support, not only boosts customer loyalty but also drives sales and brand differentiation.

Generative AI's impact on the CPG industry extends to marketing, sales, consumer research, and content creation. By automating and enhancing these functions, AI tools can significantly improve efficiency and effectiveness. The rapid generation of creative marketing content and personalized campaigns can lead to higher conversion rates and a deeper understanding of consumer preferences. Furthermore, AI's ability to quickly analyze consumer feedback and trends enables CPG companies to stay ahead of market shifts and tailor their offerings to meet evolving demands.

In an era where e-commerce is king, effective customer service is crucial. Integrating generative AI with existing AI tools can elevate customer care by automating routine inquiries and tasks, thereby allowing human agents to focus on more complex issues. This not only improves the customer experience but also optimizes operational efficiency. Generative AI can also provide valuable insights into consumer behavior, enabling companies to refine their customer service strategies and offerings.

Generative AI is a powerful catalyst for innovation within the CPG industry. Its ability to quickly generate new product designs, packaging, and marketing strategies allows companies to experiment with and launch new offerings at an unprecedented pace. This agility is critical in an industry characterized by rapidly changing consumer tastes and intense competition.

While the opportunities are vast, CPG companies must navigate several challenges to fully leverage generative AI. Issues such as ensuring the accuracy of AI-generated content, protecting against adversarial attacks, and maintaining privacy and security are paramount. Companies must implement robust quality control measures and keep humans in the loop to oversee AI operations and mitigate risks.

② Banks

The banking sector stands on the brink of a significant transformation, propelled by the advent of generative AI technologies. With McKinsey estimating a potential increase in productivity amounting to 2.8 to 4.7 percent of annual revenues, or an additional $200 billion to $340 billion, the implications of generative AI in banking extend far beyond mere financial gains. This leap in productivity is anticipated not only to enhance customer satisfaction but also to refine decision-making processes, enrich employee experiences, and fortify risk management through improved fraud detection.

Transforming Operations with Generative AI

Banks have been at the forefront of digitization, leveraging technology to streamline operations and enhance customer service. However, this reliance on technology has also resulted in a complex web of legacy systems and significant technical debt. Generative AI presents an opportunity to navigate these challenges efficiently, offering solutions that can seamlessly integrate with existing IT infrastructures while optimizing service delivery. The banking industry, characterized by its substantial customer-facing workforce and stringent regulatory environment, is uniquely positioned to benefit from generative AI's capabilities.

Key Applications of Generative AI in Banking

1. Augmenting Employee Performance with Virtual Experts: Generative AI can serve as an invaluable resource for banking professionals, offering real-time access to a wealth of proprietary knowledge. By equipping frontline employees with AI-powered assistants, banks can significantly enhance the customer experience. Morgan Stanley's deployment of an AI assistant using GPT-4 exemplifies how wealth managers can leverage generative AI to access and synthesize vast amounts of internal knowledge swiftly.

2. Streamlining Back-office Operations: The automation capabilities of generative AI can revolutionize back-office functions, reducing operational costs and improving efficiency. AI-driven chatbots, for example, can intelligently route customer requests to the most suitable service expert, ensuring that inquiries are addressed promptly and accurately.

3. Accelerating Software Development: Generative AI tools are proving instrumental in tackling the banking sector's tech debt. From drafting code to optimizing legacy systems, these tools can enhance the software development lifecycle, resulting in faster delivery times and higher-quality code.

4. Producing Tailored Content at Scale: The content generation capabilities of generative AI can significantly impact marketing and customer communication strategies. Banks can leverage these tools to create personalized content, streamline regulatory compliance processes, and ensure consistent documentation.

As banks consider integrating generative AI into their operations, several factors warrant careful consideration:

1. Regulatory Compliance: Given the heavily regulated nature of banking, any generative AI application must be compliant with existing frameworks, particularly in sensitive areas like credit risk scoring.

2. User Expectations: The diverse expectations of end-users, from employees to high-net-worth clients, must be addressed, ensuring that generative AI tools enhance rather than complicate the user experience.

3. Automation Level: Banks must decide the extent to which AI agents will operate autonomously, balancing efficiency with the need for human oversight, especially in customer interactions.

4. Data Privacy: The use of generative AI necessitates strict data governance policies to protect sensitive customer information while leveraging public data for broader insights.

The integration of generative AI into the banking sector heralds a new era of efficiency, innovation, and customer-centric services. By embracing these technologies, banks can not only overcome the limitations imposed by legacy systems and regulatory constraints but also unlock new avenues for growth and differentiation. As the industry navigates this digital transformation, the focus will remain on harnessing the full potential of generative AI to redefine banking for the digital age.

③ Pharmaceutical and medical-product

The pharmaceutical and medical-product industries are poised to experience significant transformations with the integration of generative AI. This technological advancement can catalyze efficiency and innovation in several key areas:

1. Drug Discovery and Development
Generative AI can streamline the lengthy and costly process of drug discovery and development. By automating preliminary screening in the lead identification stage, AI can rapidly sift through thousands of compounds, enhancing the selection process for promising drug candidates. This automation can drastically reduce the time from initial discovery to lead optimization, moving from several

months to just weeks.

2. Enhancing Indication Finding
Indication finding is another area where generative AI can make a substantial impact. By analyzing vast datasets of patient clinical histories and medical records, AI can identify and prioritize new indications for drugs with higher accuracy. This process involves mapping clinical events and histories to find similarities with known indications, thereby improving the success rates of clinical trials for new or repurposed drugs.

3. Accelerating Clinical Trials
Generative AI's ability to process and model massive datasets can significantly accelerate the timeline of clinical trials. By accurately identifying promising drug candidates and their potential indications, AI can streamline the trial phases, reducing the time and resources required to bring new drugs to market.

Despite these opportunities, pharmaceutical companies must navigate several challenges to fully leverage generative AI:

1. Human Oversight: The integration of AI in processes traditionally handled by humans will necessitate new quality control measures. This includes ensuring the accuracy of AI-generated content and decisions, especially in critical areas like drug discovery.

2. Explainability: The «black box» nature of some AI models can complicate efforts to understand how decisions are made. This can be problematic in contexts requiring transparency, such as regulatory compliance or when needing to trace the origins of specific findings.

3. Privacy and Security: The use of sensitive patient data raises significant privacy concerns. Companies must ensure that generative AI applications comply with regulations protecting patient information, such as HIPAA in the United States, to prevent data breaches and ensure patient confidentiality.

The potential for generative AI to revolutionize the pharmaceutical and medical-product industries is vast, promising to accelerate drug discovery, streamline clinical trials, and enhance patient care. However, realizing this potential will require careful consideration of the ethical, regulatory, and technical challenges associated with deploying AI in such a sensitive and complex domain. With thoughtful implementation, generative AI can lead to groundbreaking advancements in healthcare, benefiting patients worldwide.

The Emergence of «Safe Copilots» and the Opportunity of Integrating Their Marketplace

The landscape of digital interaction and automated assistance is undergoing a transformative shift with the advent of «safe copilots.» These advanced AI models, epitomized by platforms such as Microsoft Copilot, Google Gemini, and OpenAI's ChatGPT, are set to redefine how enterprises engage with artificial intelligence. This chapter delves into the emergence of these platforms, their significance in enhancing enterprise security paradigms, and the burgeoning opportunity that their integration into marketplaces presents.

In the nascent stages of enterprise-grade chatbots and AI assistants, apprehensions regarding data security were paramount. The crux of the concern lay in the potential for sensitive data exposure through training models with real chat transcripts or user interactions. This anxiety was not unfounded, as the confidentiality and integrity of data are cornerstones of enterprise and government operations.

However, a paradigm shift has occurred, thanks to pioneering efforts by industry leaders like Microsoft and OpenAI. Platforms such as Bing Chat Enterprise and ChatGPT Enterprise have introduced advanced safety and security measures, effectively mitigating the risk of data leaks. These measures include end-to-end encryption, stringent data access controls, and the anonymization of inputs to prevent the inadvertent training of models on sensitive information. Such advancements have not only allayed fears but also cemented the role of AI copilots as indispensable tools within enterprise architectures.

The Marketplace Opportunity: the integration of AI copilots into marketplaces in 2024 is akin to the early days of the Apple App Store—a landscape ripe with opportunity. For enterprises, the allure of being among the first to harness these platforms is twofold. First, it offers a competitive edge in leveraging AI for enhanced productivity, customer service, and decision-making. Second, it positions these enterprises at the forefront of a burgeoning ecosystem, one where the integration of AI services becomes a norm rather than a novelty.

Integrating AI copilots into an enterprise's suite of tools or services can transform various aspects of operations, from automating mundane tasks to providing real-time insights and analytics. Moreover, the «safe» aspect of these copilots—emphasizing security and privacy—makes them particularly attractive to sectors handling sensitive information, such as finance, healthcare, and government.

To capitalize on this opportunity, enterprises must consider several strategic factors:

1. Customization and Scalability: Selecting platforms that offer customization to fit specific business needs and the ability to scale with growth.

2. Interoperability: Ensuring the AI copilot can seamlessly integrate with existing enterprise systems and workflows for a unified user experience.

3. Compliance and Security: Verifying that the AI platform adheres to industry-specific regulations and standards for data protection and privacy.

4. Marketplace Dynamics: Understanding the competitive landscape within the AI marketplace and identifying potential partnerships or integration opportunities that can provide a strategic advantage.

The emergence of «safe copilots» marks a significant milestone in the evolution of AI within enterprise environments. The shift towards more secure and sophisticated AI platforms, coupled with the opportunity to integrate these services into marketplaces, presents a frontier full of potential for innovation and growth. As we move further into 2024 and beyond, the early adopters of these technologies will likely set the benchmarks for success in the digital age, redefining customer interactions, operational efficiency, and competitive strategy in the process.

After GenAI, what's the next wave?

Hype Cycle for Artificial Intelligence, 2023

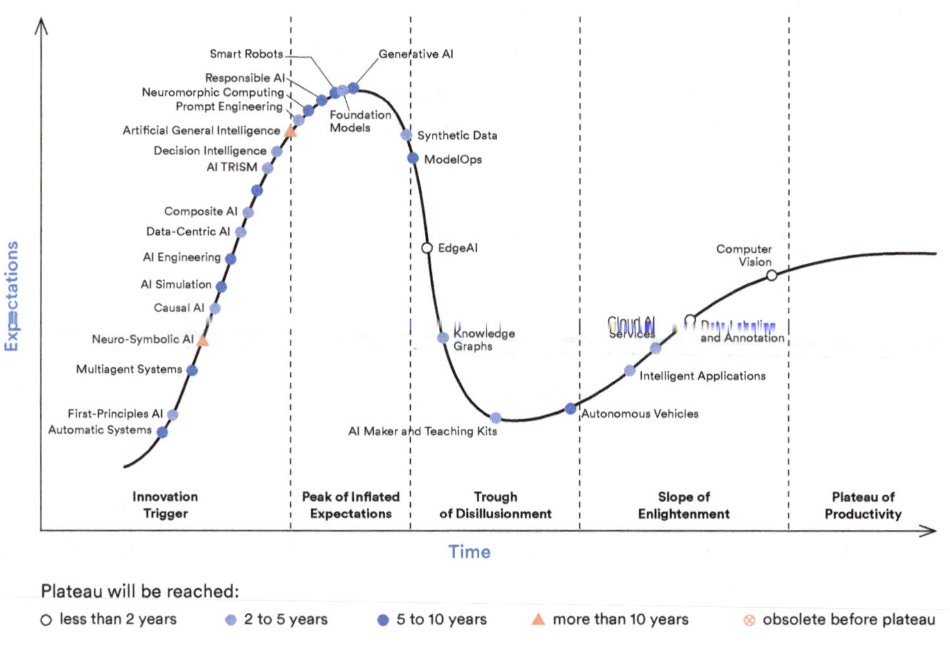

The 2023 Gartner Hype Cycle™ for Artificial Intelligence has illuminated the path towards understanding and harnessing the potential of AI innovations, particularly those surrounding generative AI (GenAI). This chapter delves into the emerging trends highlighted by Gartner, focusing on the transformative impact of GenAI and the innovations it propels and is propelled by.

The Dominance of Generative AI

Generative AI has rapidly ascended to the Peak of Inflated Expectations, a testament to its burgeoning impact across various sectors. Its ability to enhance productivity for developers and knowledge workers alike has not only optimized existing processes but also revolutionized business models and the valuation of human capital. This dual role of GenAI, both as a catalyst for and a beneficiary of technological advancements, underscores the dynamic nature of its influence.

The realm of GenAI encompasses a broad spectrum of applications, from content generation and authenticity verification to automating complex human tasks. Among the key technologies propelled by GenAI are:

- Artificial General Intelligence (AGI): Though still hypothetical, AGI represents the zenith of AI's potential, aspiring to match or surpass human cognitive abilities.
- AI Engineering: The backbone for scalable, enterprise-level AI solutions, facilitating the development and operationalization of AI systems.
- Autonomic Systems: These systems are designed for autonomy, learning, and agency, embodying the principles of self-management.
- Composite AI: By combining various AI techniques, Composite AI enhances learning efficiency and broadens knowledge representations, offering more comprehensive solutions to complex problems.
- Edge AI and Intelligent Applications: These technologies embed AI capabilities into everyday devices and applications, enabling real-time, context-aware responses.

Conversely, certain technologies serve as the bedrock upon which the advancement of GenAI is built:

- AI Simulation and Causal AI: These approaches deepen the understanding of AI agents and their interactions within simulated environments, fostering more effective and autonomous systems.
- Data Labeling and Foundation Models: The enrichment and broad training of AI models through data labeling and the development of

foundation models are crucial for advancing AI's capabilities.
- Neurosymbolic AI: This technique merges machine learning with symbolic AI, enhancing AI's reasoning capabilities and reliability.

The 2023 Gartner Hype Cycle™ for AI not only maps out the current landscape of AI innovations but also provides a glimpse into the future of technology. As we stand on the brink of this new era, organizations are encouraged to strategically adopt these innovations, navigating the hype with a keen eye on long-term viability and impact. The integration of GenAI into business processes offers a unique opportunity to redefine the competitive landscape, promising significant advantages for early adopters.

The journey towards realizing the full potential of AI is fraught with challenges, including ethical considerations, the need for robust data governance, and the imperative to ensure AI's trustworthiness. Yet, with careful planning and strategic investment, the promise of AI can be fully harnessed, paving the way for a future where AI not only augments human capabilities but also drives unprecedented innovation and growth.

Chapter 14
The Environmental Challenge of Large Language Models

In the digital age, the environmental impact of technology has become a critical issue, with Large Language Models (LLMs) like ChatGPT at the forefront of this conversation. The computational power required to train and run these models is immense, raising concerns about their sustainability. This chapter delves into the energy costs associated with LLMs, exploring the need for innovation in hardware and infrastructure optimization to mitigate their environmental footprint

Emissions when training artificial intelligence (AI) based large language models (LLMs) in 2023(in CO2 eq tonnes)

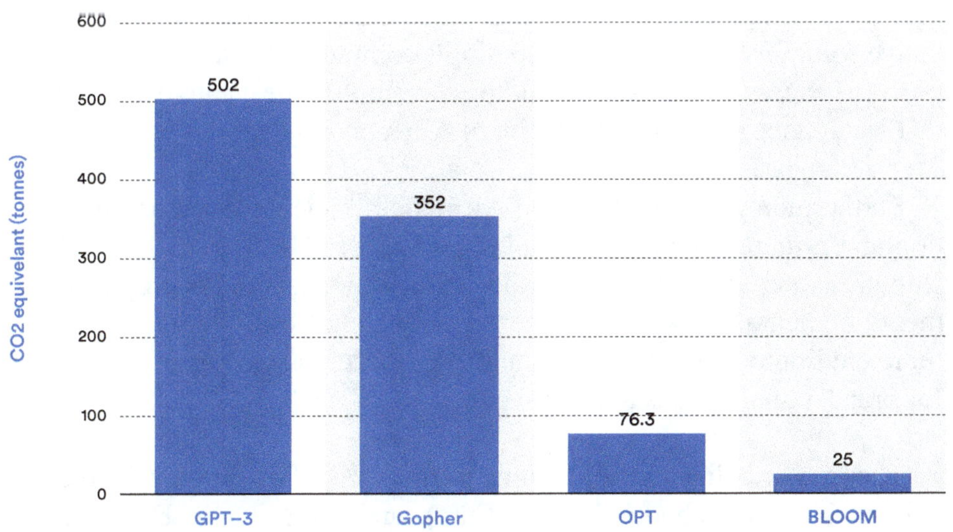

Details: Worldwide; 2022 Source: Cornell University

A pivotal study by Strubell et al. (2019) revealed the startling environmental cost of training deep learning models, equating the carbon footprint of training a single AI model to that produced by five cars over their lifetimes. This comparison starkly highlights the urgency of addressing the energy demands of LLMs. As these models grow in complexity and size, the quest for efficiency becomes even more critical. The AI and Compute analysis by OpenAI underscores this point, showing a rapid improvement in computational efficiency, with the amount of computation required to train leading AI models doubling approximately every 3.4 months.

However, the environmental challenge is not insurmountable. Innovations in hardware efficiency, such as those documented by Hugging Face with models like DistilBERT, demonstrate that it is possible to retain performance while significantly reducing energy consumption. Moreover, the shift towards renewable energy sources in data centers, exemplified by Google's achievement of matching 100% of its electricity consumption with renewable energy since 2017, offers a blueprint for sustainable AI operations.

The environmental implications of LLMs extend beyond energy consumption. The heat generated by data centers, a byproduct of running these complex models, presents both a challenge and an opportunity. Innovative solutions like Qarnot Computing's computing heaters, which repurpose this excess heat to warm buildings, exemplify the creative approaches that can reduce the carbon footprint of AI technologies.

Furthermore, advancements in AI model efficiency, such as quantization and pruning techniques detailed by Han et al. (2015) in their «Deep Compression» study, can drastically reduce the size and energy requirements of neural networks. These techniques not only make AI models more environmentally friendly but also more accessible, opening the door for broader applications and innovation.

The role of policy cannot be understated in guiding the sustainable development of AI technologies. The European Union's Green Deal and Digital Strategy, aiming for a climate-neutral Europe by 2050, underscores the importance of integrating environmental considerations into the digital sector. This regulatory framework can incentivize the adoption of green technologies and sustainable practices in AI development.

The growing public demand for sustainable and ethical AI, as highlighted by surveys from the Capgemini Research Institute, reflects a broader societal shift towards environmental responsibility. This changing landscape presents a unique opportunity for entrepreneurs and innovators to lead the charge in developing sustainable AI solutions. By focusing on the environmental challenges posed by LLMs, entrepreneurs can not only contribute to the global effort to combat climate change but also tap into a burgeoning market of eco-conscious consumers and businesses.

In conclusion, while the environmental stakes of LLMs are high, the path forward is marked by opportunities for innovation and transformation. Through concerted efforts in hardware efficiency, renewable energy adoption, and model optimization, the tech community can navigate these challenges. The environmental challenge of LLMs, far from being a deterrent, should be seen as a call to action for entrepreneurs and innovators to harness their creativity and resources towards building a more sustainable future for AI technologies.

Conclusion

As we stand on the brink of closing «Next Gen AI Founders,» it's imperative to reflect upon the journey we've embarked upon together. Through the chapters, we've traversed the expansive realms of AI capabilities, practical applications to augment ourselves and our businesses, and finally, ventured into the dynamics of building a business within the AI arena. This book has been a conduit, offering insights, methodologies, and a vision to navigate the transformative landscape of artificial intelligence in entrepreneurship.

The first part of our exploration, «AI Capabilities Unleashed,» aimed to demystify artificial intelligence, offering a solid foundation on its workings, ethical considerations, and its undeniable impact on our world. By unraveling the myths and presenting the realities, we sought to prepare you for the potential and challenges that lie ahead.

In «AI to Augment Yourself and Your Business,» the focus shifted towards tangible applications of AI. This section was designed as a toolkit, enabling you to leverage AI for optimizing operations, enhancing product development, and redefining customer experiences. The objective was clear: to showcase AI as your most formidable ally in the entrepreneurial journey.

«Build Your Business in the AI Arena» served as a clarion call to action, recognizing the vast opportunities within the AI market. This segment was crafted to guide you through the intricacies of launching and scaling an AI venture, underscored by the lessons from my own entrepreneurial journey and the booming AI industry.

As we look towards the future, my 2024 predictions for AI reflect an era of unprecedented transformation and opportunity:

- Customizable Chatbots are setting the stage for more personalized and user-driven AI experiences, enhancing interactions across platforms.
- Generative AI in Video promises to redefine the landscape of visual media, opening new horizons for content creation.
- The challenge of AI and Election Integrity underscores the urgent need for sophisticated strategies to combat AI-generated disinformation.
- Advances in Robotics are ushering in an era of more versatile and multitasking robots, impacting a myriad of sectors.
- SaaS as Conversational Agents is transforming business software interactions, making them more interactive and user-friendly.
- No-Code AI Platforms democratize the creation of AI-driven websites and apps, requiring no technical background.

In closing, I remain unwaveringly optimistic about the era we inhabit–an era adorned with tools of unparalleled power. We stand at a crossroads, and it is my firm belief that entrepreneurs, by articulating a vision and rallying teams, investors, and customers, can harness this technology for the greater good, contributing to the shaping of a better world. Through «Next Gen AI

Founders,» my hope is that you are now equipped not only to navigate the tumultuous waters of entrepreneurship with robust fundamentals but also to emerge as a Next-Gen AI Founder, augmented by artificial intelligence.

Let this book serve as your beacon, illuminating the path to innovation, resilience, and success in an AI-enhanced entrepreneurial landscape. Together, we possess the potential to forge a future where technology and human ingenuity converge, creating a legacy of progress and prosperity. Here's to becoming architects of a better tomorrow, empowered by the transformative force of AI.

Bonus
50 rules to focus your efforts and save 10 years of pain

Key Principles for Starting a Successful Startup
- Solve Real Problems: Focus on issues that people genuinely care about, ideally ones you understand and experience yourself.
- Start Small: Begin by dominating a niche market before expanding.
- Expect Challenges: Be mentally prepared for difficulties with both technology and people.
- Move Fast: Speed is crucial for learning and growth in a startup environment.

Developing Startup Ideas
- Scratch Your Own Itch: Your own experiences can be a source of ideas.
- Observe Inefficiencies: Minor annoyances can present opportunities.
- Notice Gaps in Products: Look for features or experiences that are currently lacking.
- Leverage Your Knowledge: Use your specialized expertise to identify unique problems.
- Talk to People: Different experiences can reveal unmet needs.
- Workarounds and Complaints: These often signal a demand for better solutions.

- Focus on Big Pain Points: Addressing urgent problems can lead to significant opportunities.
- Love the Problem, Not the Solution: Be open to your ideas evolving.

Building Habit-Forming Products

- Frequent Frustrations: Target problems that occur regularly.
- Immediate Value: Provide clear benefits from the first interaction.
- Simplicity: Make the product easy to use.
- Quick Interactions: Design for repeated small actions.
- Reminders and Prompts: Use triggers to encourage regular use.
- Variable Rewards: Keep users engaged with surprises.
- Leverage Natural Drives: Incorporate elements like achievement and self-expression.
- Continuous Improvement: Keep enhancing the product.

Startup Funding Strategy

- Risk Profile: Tailor fundraising to your risk tolerance.
- Milestones: Raise what you need for the next goal.
- Ramen Profitability: Aim for basic profitability early.
- Momentum: Raise larger amounts after proving traction.
- Control: Maintain decision-making autonomy.

Convincing Investors

- Market Opportunity: Show the urgency and size of the problem.
- Competitive Advantage: Explain why you'll outperform others.
- Product Appeal: Present evidence of user interest and satisfaction.
- User Stories: Share how your product has impacted users.
- Growth Plans: Highlight how you will scale.
- Mission: Convey the purpose behind your startup.

Metrics to Track

- User Growth Rate: Indicates acquisition success.
- Lifetime Value: Informs pricing and profitability.
- Churn Rate: Reflects customer satisfaction.
- Virality Rate: Measures referral growth.
- Feature Engagement: Shows what keeps users coming back.
- Funnel Conversion Rates: Identifies stages where users drop off.

Founder Mindsets

- Grit: Essential for enduring tough periods.
- Flexibility: Allows adaptation to new information.
- Tenacity: Necessary for overcoming obstacles.
- Sisu: Finnish concept embodying determination and courage.
- Delayed Gratification: Vital for long-term success.

Structuring Your Startup

- State of Incorporation: Laws and costs vary by state.
- Stock Option Pool: Allocate equity for future employees (Typical vesting schedule is 4 years with a 1-year cliff.).
- Board Composition: Ensure founders retain control initially.
- Share Classes: Determines shareholder rights.
- Protective Provisions: Gives investors certain rights.
- Founder Control: Keep majority voting power when possible.

Appendix
Quizz Scoring Sheet with Right Answers

What does AI stand for?
Correct Answer: A) Artificial Intelligence (1 point)

Name one key difference between AI and machine learning.
Correct Answer: A) AI is a broader concept that includes ML (1 point)

Can AI operate without data? Yes/No—Explain why.
Correct Answer: A) No, data is essential for AI to learn and make predictions (1 point)

What is deep learning's main architectural inspiration?
Correct Answer: A) The structure of the human brain (1 point)

Identify one task that machine learning performs better than traditional programming.
Correct Answer: A) Predictive analysis (1 point)

True or False: AI can make decisions based on emotions like humans.
Correct Answer: B) False (1 point)

What does 'training' an AI model involve?
Correct Answer: B) Exposing it to large datasets to learn from patterns (1 point)

Give an example of a task that AI can automate in a business setting.
Correct Answer: A) Scheduling appointments (1 point)

Name one limitation of AI in its current state.
Correct Answer: A) It can't experience human emotions (1 point)

What is the Turing Test designed to evaluate?
Correct Answer: B) An AI's ability to exhibit intelligent behavior

equivalent to a human (1 point)

Describe one ethical consideration when implementing AI.
Correct Answer: C) Preventing bias in AI algorithms (1 point)

Can AI create new content on its own? How?
Correct Answer: B) Yes, by learning from data and generating patterns
(1 point)

What is the role of human oversight in AI systems?
Correct Answer: B) To ensure the AI operates within ethical boundaries
and to evaluate its decisions. (1 point)

Is AI's ability to learn similar to how humans learn? Why or why not?
Correct Answer: B) No, AI learns from large datasets and specific algorithms, unlike human learning. (1 point)

True or False: AI systems are always 100% accurate.
Correct Answer: B) False (1 point)

Give an example of a problem that AI might struggle to solve.
Correct Answer: C) Understanding and replicating human empathy.
(1 point)

What is the difference between narrow AI and general AI?
Correct Answer: A) Narrow AI is designed for specific tasks, while general AI has human-like intelligence and can perform any intellectual task.
(1 point)

How does AI contribute to advancements in healthcare?
Correct Answer: C) By enhancing diagnostic procedures and
personalized medicine. (1 point)

What are some ways to address bias in AI systems?
Correct Answer: A) Use more diverse datasets. (1 point)

Where do you see AI having the most significant impact in the next decade?
Opinions may vary; however, this question helps gauge one's vision for AI's future and does not contribute to the scoring.

Scoring Method

- 1-4 Points: AI Novice
- 5-8 Points: AI Observer to AI Apprentice
- 9-12 Points: AI Implementer to AI Strategist
- 13-16 Points: AI Integrator to AI Innovator
- 17-20 Points: AI Thought Leader to AI Visionary

Interpretation

- AI Novice: You are starting to explore the vast landscape of AI, understanding its basic concepts and terminology.

- AI Observer to AI Apprentice: You recognize AI's potential and have begun to understand its principles, differentiating between AI and machine learning, and grasping foundational applications.

- AI Implementer to AI Strategist: You're equipped to apply AI solutions in practical settings, aware of ethical concerns, and can start to predict its impact on business strategies.

- AI Integrator to AI Innovator: Your proficiency allows you to seamlessly integrate AI into operations, pushing boundaries in innovative applications and understanding advanced concepts.

- AI Thought Leader to AI Visionary: You're at the forefront of AI knowledge, contributing significantly to its evolution, anticipating future trends, and understanding its potential to reshape industries globally.